CHILDCARE IN THE BALANCE

rt o Colle

Policy Studies Institute (PSI) is one of Europe's leading independent research organisations undertaking studies of economic, industrial and social policy and the workings of political institutions.

PSI is a registered charity, run on a non-profit basis, and is not associated with any political party, pressure group or commercial interest.

PSI attaches great importance to covering a wide range of subject areas with its multidisciplinary approach. The Institute's researchers are organised in groups which currently cover the following programmes:

Crime, Justice and Youth Studies – *Employment* – *Ethnic Equality and Diversity* – *Family Finances* – *Information and Citizenship* – *Information and Cultural Studies* – *Social Care and Health Studies* – *Work, Benefits and Social Participation*

This publication arises from the Work, Benefits and Social Participation Group and is one of over 30 publications made available by the Institute each year.

Information about the work of PSI and a catalogue of publications can be obtained from:
Publications Department, Policy Studies Institute, 100 Park Village East, London NW1 3SR

CHILDCARE IN THE BALANCE

How lone parents make decisions about work

Reuben Ford

POLICY STUDIES INSTITUTE

The publishing imprint of the independent
POLICY STUDIES INSTITUTE
100 Park Village East, London NW1 3SR
Tel. 0171 468 0468   Fax. 0171 388 0914

The views expressed in this report are those of the author and not
necessarily those of the Department of Social Security or any other
Government organisation or department.

ISBN 0 85374 697 4
PSI Report 823

PSI publications are available from:
BEBC Distribution Ltd, P O Box 1496, Poole, Dorset BH12 3YD

Books will normally be dispatched within 24 hours. Cheques should
be made payable to BEBC Distribution Ltd.

Credit cards and telephone/fax orders may be placed on the follow-
ing freephone numbers:
FREEPHONE   0800 262260
FREEFAX   0800 262266

Booktrade representation (UK and Eire):
Broadcast Books, 24 De Montfort Road, London SW16 1LZ
Tel. 0181 677 5129

PSI subscriptions are available from PSI's subscription agent:
Carfax Publishing Company Ltd,
P O Box 25, Abingdon, Oxford OX14 3UE

Laserset by Policy Studies Institute
Printed in Great Britain by Bourne Press Limited, Bournemouth.

Contents

LIST OF FIGURES

LIST OF TABLES

Acknowledgements

I should like to thank all those who aided and informed the production of this report as part of the Department of Social Security/Policy Studies Institute (DSS/PSI) Programme of Research Into Low Income Families (PRILIF). These include Tony Martin and Dan Murphy at the DSS and Nick Moon and Elaine Winter at National Opinion Polls Ltd. The project would not have been possible without the expert interviewing skills of Virginia Bergin, Anne Heaven, Marie Kennedy, Gill West and Jane Wilkinson. I am also grateful for the advice of an anonymous referee at the proposal stage and of Elaine Kempson, Alan Marsh, Karen Rowlingson, Louise Finlayson and colleagues at PSI.

The greatest thanks is owed to the many hundreds of lone parents who have given up their time to assist the PRILIF work.

Reuben Ford

Summary of the Main Findings

Chapter 1   The Study Question

1.1 This study looks at the extent to which lone mothers face a barrier to entering work due to the problems they face with childcare: finding suitable care and paying for it. It reports findings from a national survey of 850 lone parents carried out in late Autumn 1994 and from a depth interview follow-up in early 1995 with 57 of these lone mothers.

1.2 One of the foremost constraints on work entry among lone parents is the age of their youngest child. Where young children are present in the household, lone parents are considerably less likely to work. Childcare will be a prerequisite for most if not all lone parents of young children to take up paid work.

Chapter 2   The national study

2.1 More than one third of out-of-work lone parents say the cost of childcare constrains them from taking up work of 16 hours or more each week, and 13 per cent say it is not the cost but the availability of childcare that is the main problem. But only 5 and 2 per cent, respectively, gave these reasons *alone,* suggesting that solutions to their childcare problem may still leave these parents unable to take up work.

2.2 Among current working lone parents, just over two-thirds use childcare. The remainder work while their children are at school, work at home, take their children to work with them or leave their children at home to look after themselves.

Around three in ten working lone parents pay for their childcare (that is 42 per cent of those who use any childcare). The average amount paid was £33.20 in 1994, with half paying less than £25.00. The average cost per hour *worked* was £1.01 with 50 per cent paying less than £0.88.

2.3 Lone parents who paid for childcare paid around one fifth of their after-tax earnings in childcare costs.

2.4 Out-of-work lone parents are less likely than workers to call on the childcare services of their parents and more likely to say they would work only during school hours. Twice as many anticipate calling on the services of registered or unregistered childminders.

CHAPTER 3   ORIENTATION TO WORK AND TO FAMILY

3.1 All depth interview respondents had spent at least some time economically active, looking for work or actually in work. Typically they had been most active after they left school, and entered the world of employment before the world of partnerships and child rearing.

3.2 For those who held close to a traditional female role model of wife or partner, homemaker and child-rearer, the motivation to seek paid work was generally weaker than among those with better qualifications and a career orientation. The transition to lone parenthood tended not to change these orientations but imposed greater constraints upon their fulfilment.

3.3 Lone mothers were, of course, denied the role of wife or partner, and found the role of child-rearer diminished as children grew up. Paid employment was sought by some to provide a change of routine or social environment for lone parents who had less to occupy their days.

3.4 Many lone mothers felt their families suffered financial hardship and could be motivated to seek work for financial necessity. In such cases the financial returns from work would need to be high if work offered no other gains. The persistence of this motive among depth interview respondents was sensitive to perceived fluctuations in the returns from work.

3.5 Many in work were strongly committed to it as a life role, almost regardless of the level of remuneration.

3.6 After time out of the labour market, many lacked the skills or confidence to take up paid work. Job search was rarely a determined effort.

CHAPTER 4   IN-WORK COSTS AND WORK INCENTIVES

4.1 With the exception of mortgage-holders, who are a minority among lone parents, the benefit system is structured to preserve a financial incentive to work. The childcare disregard should maintain the financial incentive to work for lone mothers who pay for formal childcare. There may be confusion, however, among those for whom entitlement to help with childcare is delivered in the form of increased Housing Benefit and Council Tax Benefit.

4.2 Once in work of 16 hours or more, however, the incentive to work more hours can be small.

4.3 Non-workers are more likely to experience hardship (and to know that they do) than workers, but the differential was not sufficient in itself to motivate parents to seek paid work. Out-of-work lone parents not seeking work were typically worse off than those seeking it.

4.4 Lack of knowledge of the benefit system made work seem less financially attractive than it would actually be for them when in-work benefits were included.

4.5 The skills level of lone mothers not seeking work was often too low to achieve a wage rate which would make working and paying for childcare seem financially worthwhile, in the absence of knowledge about wage supplementation.

4.6 Some lone mothers who do not intend to work nevertheless had friends or relatives offering 'free' childcare.

CHAPTER 6   THE NEED FOR CHILDCARE AND CHILDCARE AVAILABILITY

6.1 The majority of lone parents were unhappy about leaving children under the age of 14 years unsupervised.

6.2 Finding formal childcare sources to cover weekends, shifts or irregular hours was very difficult. Flexibility in childcare provision is required if lone parents are to compete for jobs in a flexible labour market. Only friends or relatives offered such flexibility, and then only rarely.

6.3 In rural areas, lone parents reported a scarcity of formal childcare places.

6.4 Ill and disabled children placed additional demands on parents as the forms of suitable care available were rarely geared to working parents. These children often experienced a greater number of disruptions to their school day, reducing the ability of parents to commit time to an employer.

6.5 Depth interview respondents were divided almost equally between those for whom childcare posed a barrier to employment and those for whom it did not. A handful said childcare availability was the issue, or were deterred by a range of in-work costs among which childcare was but one. Around one third found childcare costs their primary barrier to taking up or staying in work. These parents typified those on the less favoured side of the *benefit fault-line* (Marsh, 1994). They were younger, less well qualified, less likely to receive maintenance and more likely to be tenants compared with those for whom childcare was not a barrier to employment.

CHAPTER 7   RECONCILING THE LABOUR AND CHILDCARE MARKETS

7.1 Parents with a limited knowledge of the availability or cost of childcare or of the benefit system will find it difficult to do full justice to consideration of a job vacancy. Some may err on the side of caution and remain on Income Support, others may be over-optimistic and find their in-work income package falls short of their expectations. Still others may experiment with a new job, being prepared to leave it if it doesn't work out.

7.2   Parents intending to work differed in whether they prioritised locating suitable childcare or suitable employment. Locating one would precondition the search for the other. Parents engaged in risk minimisation, seeking out first whichever element they felt was the harder to obtain.

7.3   Lone parents preferred to test out childcare arrangements before they took up work, but could not always afford to do so.

7.4   Discrimination by employers on occasion confused lone parents' priorities, since some employers demanded evidence of childcare arrangements in advance of taking up the job.

7.5   Similarly, discrimination against lone parents could impose additional constraints on job search, since lone parents found themselves restricted to finding work with the more flexible of employers.

7.6   Parents balanced the benefits of working and using childcare against the advantages of life out of work in both financial and non-financial ways. For a lone mother to avoid feeling that she is reneging on her caring role, she needed work which provided something else of equal value to her child such as a better standard of living or simply a happier mother. This was achieved either by locating care at least of a quality comparable to her own, or by balancing the shortfall in care the children experience while she is at work by using the financial returns from work to improve the quality of the remaining time the family has together.

CHAPTER 8   CHILDCARE COSTS AND AFFORDABILITY

8.1   For lone mothers, all childcare carried some cost, whether it was provided by family, friends or professionals. The cost of paid-for care could be unaffordable because its financial cost exceeded likely financial resources. The affordability of 'free' care could be judged in a parallel way through its call on a parent's emotional or human resources.

8.2 A majority of lone parents had heard of the childcare disregard, but they were less clear about how it worked.

8.3 Lone parents found it difficult to predict their likely income from income-tested benefits in work. Few know the size of the taper or the amounts of benefit they are likely to receive. Because the childcare disregard is intimately imbedded in this system, it is vulnerable to the same levels of misunderstanding.

8.4 There were few among lone parents seeking low-paid work and intending to use childcare who would see little benefit from the disregard, provided they were not disqualified by their children's ages or their preferred sources of childcare. The median predicted cost of childcare was £40 a week at the time, the same amount as the disregard. Only 20 per cent who expected to pay for childcare thought the bill would exceed £56 a week.

8.5 Parents were unhappy with the 11 year age limit on the disregard. Six in ten lone parents would want to use childcare for a 13 year-old child.

8.6 A problem with the restriction of the disregard to formal sources has also been identified. Some parents have strong preferences for informal care and a number would need to pay for such care. Most means of changing negative perceptions of formal care are beyond the reach of the benefit system, but the availability of the disregard may convince some to experiment with formal care.

8.7 The restriction to formal carers was particularly difficult for those working weekends, irregular or shift hours. The solution may rest in making informal services eligible for the disregard to cover certain hours of work, or types of work.

CHAPTER 9   CONCLUSIONS

9.1   Even in the presence of severe hardship, and regardless of the incentives to improve income offered by paid work, it must be accepted that at least some lone parents will not be motivated or able to work for at least some of the time they spend as lone parents.

9.2   In most circumstances, lone parents bear sole responsibility for any decision to change the family's status quo. Given the complexity of the decision to start paid work, and the perceived far-reaching consequences of the outcomes, they are likely to vacillate.

9.3   The problem faced by lone parents (a quarter of those interviewed) for whom childcare cost was the principal barrier to work entry is specific. They could not match the hours and rate of pay of a job vacancy to a childcare source they could then afford. For a small number of other parents, childcare costs were just part of the problem.

9.4   There was no evidence from these accounts that lone mothers faced an acute shortage of childcare, but there was evidence that parents could not guarantee the availability of affordable childcare.

9.5   Thus childcare posed some part of the problem to work entry for more than half the respondents out of work. Childcare was not a problem for the majority in work, even though the sample of workers were selected on the basis that they all paid for childcare. Childcare was a price 'career' women were prepared to pay to achieve the social, financial and career benefits work offered them. Others, for whom the financial rewards from work were fewer, had found jobs with hours which fitted the low-cost childcare they had available. Others, who saw work offering neither financial nor social returns sufficient to motivate them, were out of work. Their social world revolved around their home and family – a world in which the use of childcare carried little salience. They did the childcare. It was their job.

9.6   A final answer to the question of the childcare barrier is how much of a difference the childcare disregard may make. The more lone parents are aware of the childcare disregard, know how it works and realise that it applies to them, the more it should help those for whom childcare costs pose a problem. For it to help others, its effects must be felt far more widely. The availability of the disregard may result in improved supply – and improve the availability of affordable care. It may broaden the legitimacy of the work and childcare combination and bring greater awareness of its financial benefits. A disregard with an enlarged constituency, allowing 11, 12 and 13 year-olds the care their parents think they need, would enable many to enter work earlier than at present, and others to continue in work as their children enter their teenage years.

Chapter 1

THE STUDY QUESTION

How much, exactly, does the likely cost and availability of child-care affect the labour market opportunities of Britain's lone parent families? There may not be an exact answer to this question, but the aim of this study was to get as close as possible to an answer, using a combination of research methods, and at the same time to achieve a greater understanding of the processes involved. How do lone parents contemplating work make this complicated decision about the right job at the right time accompanied by childcare arrangements that they feel are right for them and their children? How much choice do they really have?

It is very easy to get lone parents, or women with partners for that matter, to agree that childcare is a serious barrier to paid work. Families, for example, are smaller nowadays and geographically scattered. Although this means fewer children needing care, it also means fewer relatives nearby to share family care. Alternatives that cost money will lower the cash incentive to work, especially at the kinds of wage levels most women can command in the labour market. And although they see advantages in work, few women will say there are no disadvantages in substituting their own care with another's.

Yet despite these 'obvious' childcare barriers to work, the labour market participation of all women with dependent children has more than doubled from just three in ten to two-thirds in the last 25 years. It is one of the more remarkable transformations in British society and the proportion of working mothers continues to rise (Sly, 1994). Even a fifth of those with pre-school children now work 16 or more hours a week. The paradox is that none of this happened because the supply of childcare was dramatically increased. What policies were put into action actually restricted the supply of childcare by requiring the registration of child-minders and the discouragement of unregulated forms.

Certainly, many working mothers mobilised their partners for childcare, particularly in support of part-time work or in covering for after-school care for older children. Lone parents were mostly denied this option, though small but increasing numbers name a 'partner' as helping with childcare (Finlayson, Ford and Marsh, 1996 forthcoming). How do they solve their problem? It is lone parents' more difficult choices – choices contemplated amid numbers of other difficulties such as a lack of education, training or experience – that this study was designed to untangle.

It has become part of conventional wisdom that problems arranging and paying for childcare account for a great deal of lone parents' absence from the labour market (Bradshaw and Millar, 1991; Holtermann, 1993). This report sets out to explore this hypothesis fully, using quantitative analysis of data from a large-scale survey of 880 lone parents conducted in Autumn 1994 (the 'National Survey') and qualitative analysis of follow-up depth interviews with 57 of these lone parents (the 'Depth Study').

However, to explore the childcare hypothesis, the constraints imposed by the cost and availability of childcare must be considered in the context of all the other constraints. Is childcare an issue that simply overrides all the others, that it is just not worth confronting all the other problems of getting suitable work while no obvious solution to childcare seems in sight? Or are childcare difficulties more often a 'last straw' that turns an otherwise difficult but soluble set of constraints into an impossible one. If they did not have children at all, would they be in work? Childcare could be just one of a number of factors.

With this wider remit in mind, the remainder of this chapter prepares the ground for Chapter 2 which considers the evidence from a recent national survey of lone parents and for the Depth Study results which form the main text of this report (from Chapter 3) as follows:

- the policy context of lone parents' labour participation decisions;

- a discussion of lone parents' orientation to the labour market: their motivation to work and the incentives they see;

- a review of existing research on lone parents' labour market activity.

THE POLICY CONTEXT

The financial circumstances of lone parents have been a major focus of the DSS/PSI Programme of Research Into Low Income Families (PRILIF), which began with a study of the role played by the in-work benefit, Family Credit, in helping families get and keep paid work. One of the most striking findings from this 'Families, Work and Benefits' study (Marsh and McKay, 1993b) was obtained even before the main interviews were under way. Sift data on incomes revealed that although lone parent families constituted one fifth of Britain's families with dependent children, they represented half of those families with low incomes.[1] Nine out of ten lone parent families met this low-income definition. Five in every six lone parent families rely on means-tested benefits: two-thirds claim Income Support, and one in six claim Family Credit. In the 1991 and later interview surveys, claiming means-tested benefits was closely related to being found in severe material hardship (McKay and Marsh, 1994; Ford, Marsh and McKay, 1995).

Government policy is to help families improve their standard of living by increasing independent sources of income: largely earnings and maintenance. The latest PRILIF survey estimates that earnings and maintenance together contributed 28 per cent of lone parents' incomes in 1994. A succession of changes to benefit rules, following on from the introduction of Family Credit, reflect this policy:

- 1992: reduction in the minimum number of hours worked to qualify for Family Credit from 24 to 16 each week; disregard of the first £15 of maintenance received each week in income assessed for Family Credit.
- 1993: introduction of the Child Support Agency to regularise and enforce child maintenance payments commensurate with absent parents' means.
- 1994: disregard of the first £40 spent each week on professional childcare for children aged under 11 years in family income assessed for in-work benefits.
- 1995: introduction of a weekly £10 bonus payment to Family Credit claimants working 30 hours or more.
- 1996: increase in the childcare disregard to £60 each week.

Evidence from the DSS/PSI cohort study of lone parents suggests that movement into work, or an increase in income through other means – receiving more maintenance or marrying an employed partner – is associated with improved family welfare. A policy which aims to raise living standards through securing access to an independent source of income for the family will succeed in most cases.

Whilst the Child Support Agency (CSA) has been successful in increasing the size of maintenance payments for some, and bringing some lone parents into receipt of child support for the first time, still only three in ten lone parents were receiving maintenance in 1994 – the same fraction as in previous years since 1989.

The other route out of hardship is entry into paid employment. Policy is explicitly focused on removing barriers to taking up paid employment (DSS, 1995). The most recent policy changes, especially the reduction in the weekly hours needed to place a claim for Family Credit and the childcare disregard, have been aimed at making employment more attractive to parents for whom finding someone to care for their children while they work poses a particular problem. The 1992 changes in benefit rules provide greater scope for taking up employment solely within school hours. The hours rule change made longer part-time hours particularly attractive to lone parents. Six in ten lone parents working 16 to 23 hours each week and interviewed less than a year after the rule change said they had started a new job at those hours as a result of the change (Ford, Marsh and McKay, 1995). The modal number of hours worked among lone parent Family Credit claimants is now just 16 and the average is 25.

The initial popularity of combining shorter hours of work and Family Credit as recorded in 1993, persisted in 1994, but the proportion working more than 23 hours fell back from 26 to 20 per cent. Accompanying the growth in the numbers of lone parents, the number of lone parents on Income Support continues to increase: consistently two-thirds of the total. What is it that acts to keep half of Britain's lone parents out of the labour market altogether, and two-thirds out of work of 16 hours or more?

WHY ARE LONE PARENTS NOT IN WORK?

There are many hypotheses as to why so few lone parents enter the labour market. They embrace an interrelated range of attitudinal and structural factors. These include the willingness of women to enter paid employment and their ability to do so, the opportunities open to them and the perceived financial incentive offered by paid work.

Willingness or motivation to work is the key issue. Any explanation of what keeps lone parents out of the labour market must ask whether the labour market is somewhere lone parents would like to be: what benefits and disadvantages do they feel it offers them? But other factors influence motivation to work and may act as constraints upon those who want to work. Without the development of a motivation to work, however, entry into employment is unlikely to be successful.

Official terminology derives, in part, from a recognition of the motivation to work. It is inappropriate to use the term 'unemployed' to refer to lone parents unless they themselves say they are 'unemployed and seeking work' as just 5 to 7 per cent say they are. Along with other parents, they perform the valuable task of raising the future generation. And most out-of-work lone mothers do so without the immediate intention of combining the task with paid work, as do three in ten women in couples but only one per cent of men. The absence of the requirement for the parent-with-care to be seeking work when claiming Income Support means most out-of-work lone parents are better described as looking after home and family.

Debates surrounding lone parents' decisions to work have focused less on motivation and more on incentives. A particular focus has been on the disincentives engendered by childcare costs and the benefit system on part-time work (Blundell, 1994). The availability of Family Credit means lone parents have considerably higher incomes (an average of £30 more each week) in full-time work than they would have out of work, even on their traditionally low rates of pay (McKay and Marsh, 1994). It is argued that the effect of changes in wage rates and of in-work benefits is seen largely to influence lone parents' decisions about whether or not to participate, rather than to change the number of hours they work (Blundell, 1994).

Such theories clearly set aside the question of motivation to work. Yet it must be acknowledged that incentives apply only to those who intend to work. Most likely there is a trade-off between incentives and motivation. People's motivation to work will change with their perceptions of the rewards from employment. Thus, increasing the monetary and non-monetary incentives offered by paid work will alter the relative value of different life roles and consequently behavioural intentions. Even this neo-classical economic perspective – that everyone has their price – recognises the imperfections introduced when people at particular points in their lives simply cannot contemplate working.

One of the reasons why incentives have been the focus of so many commentaries is because they form the main focus of policy. Most of the policy changes with the stated aim of removing the barriers to paid work are focused on increasing the financial return from taking paid work of 16 or more hours each week compared to working fewer or none at all.

For those lone parents who are prepared to work, the incentives issue can be regarded as an equation (Duncan, Giles and Webb, 1995). Those out of work are assumed more likely to be tempted in if the margin between the financial returns from working and not working can be increased. If the monetary reward from work is raised, the balance is assumed to tip in favour of employment:

$$\text{utility of work} + \text{utility of childcare} \geq \text{cost of}$$
$$\text{being in work} + \text{cost of childcare}$$

This balance analogy is a useful one since it implies an equation in which the advantages and disadvantages of working are balanced against the pros and cons of life out of work. Parents are unlikely to be equipped with sufficient information to solve this equation precisely, but the equation analogy acts as a useful device with which childcare can be ascribed a role in the decision-making process. Its financial cost can be taken into account, and so can non-financial gains and losses: for example in the quality of care, separation of the family and the inconvenience of organising childcare.

THE ROLE OF CHILDCARE IN THE DECISION TO WORK: EXISTING KNOWLEDGE

One of the constraints on lone parents' entry into paid work which cuts across the incentives and motivation debate is childcare. Attempts to reduce lone parents' childcare costs are clearly focused on increasing the financial return from work. Yet their preparedness to use childcare and the types of childcare which they have access to and are prepared to use, are rooted in their perceptions of their own life role and of their role in their children's lives. In other words, whether they see themselves as provider, carer or both.

The decision to work is closely linked to a judgement about the number of hours that can be worked. This, in turn, is associated with the relative value to mothers of economic gains versus time spent at home with children, or in other activities. Mothers will place a value on the use of childcare itself, independent of its role in supporting work entry, based on its relative benefit to the child. Although women's decisions to work have been subject to extensive research, attempts to explain how parents balance gains from work with those of having and caring for children, by modelling their behavioural differences, remain inconclusive (Berger and Black, 1992; Connelly, 1992; Holtermann, 1992; Joshi and Davies, 1993).

Models of future participation (for example, Holtermann, 1992) have encountered basic methodological problems. Some models predict women's future economic behaviour from their answers to questions which propose a hypothetical future scenario (for example, of universally available childcare). In addition, forecasts of economic activity cannot be simply translated into rates of participation and hours worked without knowledge of future labour demands and workers' preferences independent of the childcare issue.

The more children a lone parent has, the less likely she is to be found in employment (Bradshaw and Millar, 1991). The presence of young children is a particular deterrent (McKay and Marsh, 1994). A problem is thus posed for modelling if, as highlighted by Connelly (1992), the number of children parents choose to have is not independent of their labour participation decisions. Mothers who are less inclined to take paid work may also be inclined to have more children, and thus be overrepresented within cross-sections of mothers with young children. Models may thus overestimate the negative effect of having young children on the decision to take paid work.

It is also difficult to use historical evidence to argue that increases in women's participation necessarily follow a reduction in the cost of childcare or an increase in provision. The economic participation rates of women with dependent children have more than doubled since the mid-1960s, but this has been achieved over a period of very little public investment in care facilities. Even recent initiatives, such as the introduction of nursery vouchers for four year-olds, offer no guarantee of additional places, nor of the availability of places to those in low-paid work.

The effect of policy changes over time must be considered alongside changing attitudes within each cohort of new families. Parents differ in their perceptions of what constitutes suitable or acceptable childcare. The British Social Attitudes Survey found three in five mothers would prefer their child to be cared for by a relative, although many more mothers feel nurseries to be suitable for their children than are able to use one (Witherspoon and Prior, 1991). Some look to nurseries to improve the socialisation of their children while others feel the quality of care is better in less formal settings where carers have more time for each child. If the state subsidises use of only regulated childcare, this may induce a *reduction* in the number of hours worked as parents who change to using day nurseries forsake some paid work to continue former levels of informal care provision themselves (see Berger and Black, 1992).

Many mothers prefer to remain out of employment for extended periods. According to the British Social Attitudes Survey, a majority of mothers say that they will only work when their children are at school. The survey found that, given the childcare arrangements of their choice, two-thirds of mothers not in paid work would go out to work, but that 80 per cent of them would work only part-time. Furthermore, under such conditions, a quarter of those working full-time would choose to work fewer hours (Witherspoon and Prior, 1991). In 1990, an OPCS survey of day care found the mothers of fewer than half the pre-school children surveyed who preferred to use formal care services (day nursery, playgroups, nursery class or school) cited their ability to go to work as a reason for preferring such care (Meltzer, 1994).

Each successive survey of lone parents in Britain has identified factors associated with childcare as important in lone mothers' decisions about work. In 1989, one third of lone mothers on Income Support said that difficulties with childcare were the main reason why they were not working (Bradshaw and Millar, 1991). Half of these difficulties were associated with the cost of childcare ('costs too much', 'cannot afford to pay') and one third with the availability of suitable care ('lack of availability', 'dislikes strangers'). A regular observation is that it is lone parents' problems with childcare that keep them out of the labour market and hence out of work and on Income Support.

> If all the lone mothers who said they wanted to work now were able to do so, then lone mothers would have almost exactly the same employment rates as married mothers. If those who said they did not want to work now but who would return to work sooner if they had childcare could also find jobs and childcare, then about seven in ten lone mothers would be employed. There is thus a lot of untapped potential for employment, and many lone mothers now on Income Support would welcome an opportunity to take paid work. (Bradshaw and Millar, 1991:47)

Findings from a survey of lone parents two years later suggested a continuing if less prominent role for childcare. Among lone parents without paid work in 1991, four out of five said they might return to work 'one day' (McKay and Marsh, 1994). More than half of these did not expect to return to work within a year or so. A smaller proportion than in 1989, one in five, gave reasons associated with childcare.

An important caveat in considering the constraint childcare places on decisions about work is that the need for childcare does not persist indefinitely: other factors must be acting to make half these parents unwilling to return to work beyond the short-term. These include each woman's perceptions of her role in life and of what the labour market has to offer. Many lone parents who say childcare poses difficulties also report other constraints on working. It is apparent already from these data that while childcare may present an immediate and intractable problem for some, it is far from the only reason keeping lone parents out of work.

Thus, for an issue that is said so often to be 'obvious' it is far from clear to what extent improving the provision of childcare or reducing its cost to lone parents would increase the proportion in work.

ANSWERING THE STUDY QUESTION

This study looks at the extent to which lone parents face a barrier
to entering work of more than just part-time hours due to the
problems they face with childcare: finding suitable care and paying
for it. It aims to identify the likely customer base among lone
parents for policy changes aimed at making childcare cheaper. In
doing so, it builds upon a strong tradition of research into lone
parents' labour market decisions.

In answering the question, the discussion will frequently refer
to the *affordability* of childcare as distinct from its *cost*.
Affordability is a concept which goes beyond the pounds per week
charged for the care, and even the strict financial equation of
expenditure not exceeding available income. The dictionary definition of to afford is 'to be able to do or spare something without
incurring financial difficulties or without risk of undesirable consequences'. Thus affordability is associated with current or perceived
likely income in work, to the extent that costs can be met without
incurring hardship. The concept also embraces non-financial elements: do the net benefits of working *and* of using childcare outweigh the net benefits of staying at home? The dual nature of
affordability and the requirement for lone parents to weigh up
financial and non-financial benefits adds further to the complexity
of the decision to enter work.

So what is the scope for encouraging lone parents into work by
offering to meet some of their childcare costs? The answer to this
question is dependent on answers to several intermediate questions:

- Who, among lone parents, is motivated to work?
- Who, among those not motivated, would change their outlook
  in the context of cheaper or more widely available, suitable
  childcare?
- Who, among those so motivated, is constrained from work
  entry primarily by the cost of childcare?

First, we must identify for whom, among lone parents, the cost
and/or availability poses a significant barrier to their taking or
remaining in work. If other barriers are also in the way, altering
the cost of childcare will not be sufficient in itself to change labour
market behaviour. Thus, childcare costs will be irrelevant to those

who are not motivated to work, or who are permanently sick or disabled. And even for those who want to work, if childcare costs act alongside other constraints, such as an absence of suitable jobs, then solving the childcare problem will still not necessarily enable the lone parent to enter work.

For some, whose negative perceptions of the returns to working contribute to their low motivation to seek employment, changes in the extent to which suitable childcare is available or affordable may change the motivation to work. So this study must examine not only lone parents' reasons for not working but what their orientation is towards work and how the availability and affordability of childcare influences that perspective.

Thus the study must identify lone parents for whom the cost and availability of childcare is either the sole barrier to work entry or for whom the removal of such barriers would change their orientation to the labour market sufficiently for them to start seeking work.

STRUCTURE OF THE REPORT

Chapter 2 presents findings from the National Survey of lone parents. Chapters 3–9 concentrate on Depth Study results. These chapters first set the context in which lone parents differentially affected by the cost and availability of childcare can be identified. This involves assessing first the extent of lone mothers' orientation to work and to family, including an examination of their employment history. This picture of mothers' motivation to work will be complemented in Chapter 4 by a consideration of the extent of the perceived incentive to work. Chapters 5 and 6 examine the range of factors which influence the range of childcare options parents perceive, the need for childcare and its local availability. By the end of Chapter 6, we can identify those for whom the cost and availability of childcare is the major constraint on entering and staying in work, those for whom it is only one of many concerns, and those lone mothers for whom the childcare issue is largely irrelevant. The answer to the study question comes from explaining membership of each group. Four groups of lone mothers are identified:

A   those for whom the affordability of childcare is the major barrier to entering or staying in work (including one for whom cost would be an issue were it not for her agoraphobia, and one other who simply cannot contemplate paying for care and is consequently not seeking work) (n=15);

B   those who identify childcare as part of a group of in-work costs (housing costs, travel, clothing) which reduce their incentive to work (n=4);

C   those who identify the availability of suitable care as the problem, but not its cost (n=10);

D   those for whom childcare cost/availability is not a problem (this is a broad group ranging from those who do not want or expect to be able to work and those who doubt that they could earn enough to make a job worth doing, irrespective of the issue of childcare, to those who earn so much that childcare cost is immaterial). This group includes people who have problems with childcare, but crucially no one who is stopped from working by its cost or availability (n=28).

To aid interpretation of interview extracts and quotations, the pseudonyms of respondents have been coded by initial letter to indicate group membership and employment status (Table 1.1). Throughout the report, therefore, the reader will be able to build up a picture of each respondent which should aid the explanation of group membership in Chapter 6.

From Chapter 7 onwards, with a view to the implications for policy (Chapter 9), more applied aspects of the childcare problem are considered. Chapter 7 examines how lone parents solve problems locating childcare and matching it to work demands. Chapter 8 addresses how parents evaluate the benefits and disadvantages of using childcare and working and how they arrive at conclusions about its affordability. It also looks at awareness of the childcare disregard and where it fits into the process of finding work and locating suitable childcare.

Note

1   Low-income families were defined as those whose incomes failed to exceed 125 per cent of their family's threshold for Family Credit. This definition incorporates the equivalising scale built into the Family Credit system. All families on Income Support and Family Credit fall into this group.

Table 1.1 Respondent pseudonyms and group membership codes

	A	B	C	D
Employment status at time of interview	Affordability of childcare is the issue	In-work costs of childcare is the issue	Availability of childcare is the issue	Neither availability nor cost of childcare is the issue
In work 16+ hours each week	Tanya Tracy	Alison	Carrie** Cathy Claire Cynth*	Steph Sasha Shirley* Samantha** Sue Sonia** Sian** Sharon Sophie* Sarah Susan Sandra Sadie Sally*
Not in work 16+ hours each week	Maureen** Maxine May Maggie** Maria Michelle Marsha* Meg Melanie** Mary Margaret Marion* Marie**	Rebecca Ruth* Rachel	Elaine Esther Elizabeth Ellie Eileen Emma	June Janice Jane Jill Jackie* Jess Josie Julie** Janine** Judith Joanna Jenny* Janet Jean**

*   denotes parents of a child with long-term or limiting illness or disability
** denotes where these children require additional care

Chapter 2

The National Study

This chapter presents results of an analysis of new national data on the importance of childcare prospects in seeking or not seeking work. It compares what is known about working lone parents' actual use of childcare and the childcare out-of-work lone parents expect to use if they entered work. In doing so, it suggests variation between parents in the importance placed on childcare to explaining their economic activity. It is these differences which the more detailed depth interview investigation in later chapters seeks to explain.

What role does childcare currently play?

The study set out to determine how important childcare is in lone parents' labour market decisions. A useful starting place is to look at what characterises lone parents who work 16 hours or more from those who do not, whether they use and pay for childcare, and how much they pay. For this analysis, we concentrate on data from the 1994 DSS/PSI National Survey of lone parents – the same group of lone parents from which the sample interviewed for the Depth Study was drawn.

A common reason for assigning a strong explanatory role to childcare problems is the low participation rate observed among mothers of young children. The study's first report (Marsh, Ford and Finlayson, 1996 forthcoming) contained a modelling exercise in which the independent effect of several factors felt to influence labour market participation, including age of the youngest child, were tested. The logistic regression analysis allowed effects to be tested independently of one another (Table 2.1). For example, receiving maintenance was found to increase participation by the same magnitude as having 'O' level qualifications or better.

All else being equal, the first four effects in Table 2.1: being ill, having a child aged under 5 years, having more than two children and renting from a local authority or housing authority, reduced the probability of being in work compared to their null categories (being well, having only children aged five years or older, having only one or two children and not being a social tenant). Being in receipt of maintenance, being an owner with a mortgage and being qualified to 'O' level or above improved the chances of participation.

Table 2.1 Predicted probabilities of work: part-time and full-time

percentages

		Probability of working	
	full-time (24+ hours)	16+ hours	any work
Reference	16	29	42
As reference, but long-term sick or disabled	4	6	14
As reference, youngest aged 0-4 years	6	12	19
As reference, 3 or more children	7	18	27
As reference, social tenant	9	19	38 NS
As reference, divorced	15 NS	21 NS	39
As reference, but receiving £1+maintenance	22 NS	43	51
As reference, owner occupier with mortgage	29	53	75
As reference, with 'O' levels or better	33	44	49 NS

Note: NS = Not statistically significant at 95 per cent level of confidence

The reference category is a lone parent, receiving no maintenance, who has only one child, aged 11-15 years, is separated from a cohabitation, a private tenant, and has no educational qualifications.

This type of analysis helps us to disentangle the constraints on work entry. It becomes clear that foremost among these is the health of the parent and, indeed, the age of the youngest child. The latter difference overrides often-quoted age and marital status differences in labour market participation.

As lone parent families with young children are almost by definition required to make use of childcare if they are to go out to work, differentials such as those presented in Table 2.1 are often taken as evidence that the key to improving labour market participation is through improvements in the affordability and availability of childcare. Such a conclusion, however, rests on the assumption that childcare is the only constraint acting on mothers of preschool children, and that many more actually want to work than do so.

In the absence of data about the *availability* of childcare to individual families, this analysis of current employment status is unable to take the debate about the role of childcare further.

A more complete picture might be expected to emerge when lone parents themselves are asked directly what problems they face when considering work and when applying for jobs. The 1994 survey directed questions to those out of work about the constraints, if any, they perceived on their ability to go out to work. This question was not asked of those who had been recently seeking work, on the assumption that factors such as the availability of childcare were not acting to stop them from working. It was asked of the 10 per cent of lone parents who could not see themselves returning to work, even 'one day'. But the responses of this group are omitted from Table 2.2 since it seems unlikely such respondents could envisage their circumstances in work or would be influenced immediately by policy changes.[1] Respondents gave answers in their own words (as many answers as they wished) which were allocated by interviewers to pre-defined response categories on the questionnaire. Other answers were coded separately.

Among those who could see themselves returning to work 'one day', the most common reason given for not working at present was having children who were too young. If this answer is taken at face value it means parents felt their children were too young to be apart from their mother, or to use childcare. Although the answer could be associated in some cases with a lack of suitable childcare, the face value answer is accepted for now. Two-thirds of those who answered in this way had at least one child under five years. The next most common reason was not being able to afford childcare. This was the most common reason among those who had undertaken work of 16 or more hours in the recent past. However, parents with children aged under five years were no more likely to give this reason than those whose youngest child was aged between five and ten, and were *less* likely to state problems with the availability of care. This is further evidence that low participation rates among parents of young children cannot be accounted for solely by childcare problems. Nearly one in five said that they were better off not working, rising to one in four among those who had spent more than three years out of work, and one in three among those whose youngest child was of secondary school age.

Table 2.2 Reasons for not working 16 or more hours each week at present among lone parents not working 16+ hours in 1994*

	% giving reason (multiple response)	% giving this reason *alone*	% giving reason who have worked 16+ hrs since April 1991	% of those who have worked 16+ hrs giving reason	% of those out of work since 1991 giving reason
Cannot afford childcare	36	5	30	48	38
No childcare available	13	2	27	15	13
Children too young	41	18	23	42	37
Illness/disability	11	6	21	10	14
No work available	15	4	17	11	20
Better off not working	26	9	18	21	28
No reason	6	5	21	6	5
Other	19	7	11	10	24
n =	365	201	82	82	202

* excludes those who have sought work in the past 12 months and those who cannot see themselves looking for a paid job of 16 or more hours each week even 'one day'.

Although only one in five with recent experience of working 16 or more hours each week explicitly referred to the lack of a financial incentive, half said they could not afford childcare, suggesting many more might be in work if the financial rewards from work were sufficient to help pay for their childcare.

The availability rather than the cost of childcare and, indeed, the availability of work itself, did not feature prominently among answers. Lone parents did not envisage major problems finding work. Fewer than one in ten of those with pre-school children or children of secondary school age saw finding work as a problem. One in four of those whose youngest child was aged between five and ten did state such problems: perhaps a reflection of their (failed) attempts to find work of suitable hours once their children started school. However, those who had actually been looking for work in the past year, who are likely to have a more realistic knowledge of the state of the labour market, are excluded from this analysis (but see below).

Lone parents were able to give multiple answers to this question, and half gave more than one answer: 365 respondents gave a total of 611 reasons for not being in work. The second column of Table 2.2 shows the proportion who gave just one reason for being out of work. *Thus, for only 5 per cent was the cost of childcare the only constraint on them entering work, and for just 2 per cent was it the availability of childcare.* For 8 per cent either or both of these problems existed, but no other. These one in twelve who cited childcare problems alone differed little in their characteristics from other lone parents out of work: just one fifth received maintenance from a former partner, for example, and half had children aged five years or younger. As their unweighted number was just 18, it is difficult for any characteristics which distinguish them from other out of work lone mothers to be identified. Eleven of the 18 lived in small towns or rural areas, compared to 40 per cent of other lone parents. Small industrial towns outside the South East – for example, Darwen, Pontypool, Neath, Carlton (S. Yorks), Sandal, Easington – were over-represented.

For six in every seven of those citing problems with childcare, there was another problem which would also have to be solved before the lone parent could enter work. This is evidence to suggest that solving lone parents' childcare problems in isolation will not necessarily remove all barriers to their return to work. The reasons which were most commonly cited as a sole barrier to work were illness and disability, and having children who were too young.

Nonetheless, the boundaries between these answers are subtle and open to interpretation. A lone parent who cannot afford childcare costs could also say that such costs meant it was not worth her while working. She might give both reasons but find her problems solved by a single solution: a change which made her able to afford her childcare. One who stated she could not work because her children were too young might say so because she could not envisage suitable childcare being available for her children. These definitional problems arise because lone parents can perceive objectively similar problems in different ways, and a single question on a pen and paper questionnaire cannot pick up the complexities of how each parent arrived at their decision.

The extent of childcare problems among job-seekers

Lone parent job-seekers, by definition, could not argue that childcare problems stopped them looking for work. Hence the above analysis concentrated on those who had not sought work in the past year. But childcare problems could also affect those who sought work, either preventing them from applying for jobs with certain hours or rates of pay, or preventing them from taking up job offers.

Among lone parents who were not working 16 or more hours each week at the time of interview, nearly a quarter (23 per cent) had been seeking work at some point during the past 12 months, and of these two-thirds were still seeking work at the time of interview. Those with recent work experience were much more likely to be represented among the job seekers. Four in ten of those who had been working 16 or more hours a week in the past three years were searching, as were a third of those who had lost part-time jobs, and 22 per cent of those in part-time jobs. Only one in six of those who had been out of work continually since 1991 had been seeking work in the past year.

Of those currently not in work of 16 or more hours each week who had sought a job of these hours, six in ten had applied for at least one job. Of these, 18 per cent had been successful in that they had gained employment, and also unsuccessful since by definition they had lost the job by the time of interview. The most common single reason (for one fifth) was being made redundant, but one in six had taken the work on as a short-term contract. Only three lone parents (6 per cent) cited a breakdown in childcare arrangements.

These data allow us to estimate the success of lone parent job searches. We add to those lone parents considered above the 25 lone parents who entered their current work of 16 or more hours each week in the past year, 18 of whom had also been seeking work and who had, by definition, been successful in their application. A total of 182 lone parents (20 per cent of the sample) were not in work of 16 or more hours each week a year ago but searched for such work at some point in the past year. Of these, 62 per cent actually applied for a job. One fifth entered work at those hours (30 per cent of applications). These parents whose applications were successful were more likely to have been married to their former partner, and more likely to live in urban rather than rural areas. They were no more likely than those who were unsuccessful to have a driving licence and qualifications at 'O' level or above, and *less* likely to have qualifications at 'A' level or above. Of all the original seekers, just 10 per cent (56 per cent of those who got a job) kept their jobs to the time of interview. Those most successful at keeping in work were younger, better qualified and more likely to hold a driving licence. There was little evidence that health status or tenure as recorded at the time of interview influenced likelihood of getting work or staying in work.

Of those whose applications were turned down, four in ten were not given a reason. Among those who were, one in seven were told they lacked the experience necessary – but none that they lacked suitable qualifications – 6 per cent were told they were too old and a quarter were given other reasons. For 9 per cent, the employer withdrew the vacancy, while 7 per cent decided not to take the job after all. *Childcare did not feature among their reasons.*

Only eight out-of-work lone parents failed to apply for a job they had intended to apply for. Two said this was because they felt they lacked the experience necessary and two felt that they would not be able to afford the childcare. The remaining four gave other reasons.

Those currently out of work who had stopped seeking work within the past year were asked what was stopping them looking for work. Four in ten said it was because they were better off not working, a quarter said they could not afford childcare, and one in six said their children were too young. None of the parents who gave this last answer had a child younger than two years, or knew themselves to be pregnant. Perhaps children's ages only arose as an issue once the requirements of a particular vacancy became more tangible.

Thus, among job-seekers, childcare featured as a reason for one fifth absenting themselves from the labour market, but was rarely a reason for forsaking a suitable vacancy. Of course, we have yet to find out the extent to which being able to locate and afford suitable childcare influences or conditions what vacancies a lone parent deems suitable.

Use of childcare among workers

A substantial proportion of lone parents are able to work and find some way of looking after their children. One way to assess how important childcare is to lone parents is to examine how those in work use and pay for childcare. While the same childcare solutions may not apply to currently out-of-work lone parents (because in-work and out-of-work lone parents may not share access to the same types of jobs or childcare), the following analysis gives some idea of how other lone parents manage arrangements for looking after their children while they work.

Table 2.3 gives a breakdown of the term-time childcare used by lone parents currently working or in their most recent job. Sources are concentrated among family and friends, with a minor role played by each of the 'formal' sources, payment for which might qualify for the childcare disregard (sources marked in bold).

Among current working lone parents, just over two-thirds use childcare. The remainder work while their children are at school, work at home, take their children to work with them or leave their children at home to look after themselves. Around three in ten working lone parents pay for their childcare (that is 42 per cent of those who use any childcare). The mean amount paid per week was £33.20 in 1994, with half paying less than £25.00 per week. The average cost per hour *worked* was £1.01 with 50 per cent paying less than £0.88. Costs were considerably higher if there were more than two children in the family, if the lone parent worked part-time (fewer than 16 hours each week) and if the youngest child was aged under five years (mean cost £1.19 per hour) (Finlayson, Ford and Marsh, 1996 forthcoming). Childcare costs – where incurred – averaged 20 per cent of net earnings.

Lone parents can use many different sources of childcare. Those who use formal childcare are much more likely to pay for their childcare than those who use informal sources. The data do not permit a breakdown by source, but if it is assumed that where lone parents use formal sources and pay for care then at least some of that payment goes to the formal source, the proportions paying for each source in the central section of Table 2.3 are obtained. Registered childminders, day nurseries, after-school schemes, crèches and nannies were nearly always paid for, but fewer than half had to pay for use of a nursery school or playgroup. More were found paying who used only informal care: unregistered childminders and relatives/friends.

Table 2.3 All lone parents who have worked since 1991: childcare in most recent or current job, termtime

	All %	All currently working 16+ hrs %	% of those using each form of care who pay/paid for: **formal care**	informal care	% who have an alternative source
Ex-partner	8	5	1	19	66
Parents (in law)	25	29	4	14	64
Siblings	5	4	4	12	54
Other relatives/friends	18	14	4	46	66
Nursery/crèche	3	3	91	-	56*
Nursery school/playgroup	2	2	43	-	51
Registered childminder	7	2	87	-	65
Unregistered childminder	4	4	13	75	50
Live in nanny/Au pair	1	0	100	-	100
Other daily/shared nanny	0	1	50	-	50
After school scheme	1	2	81	-	75
Non-childcare					
I only work during school hours	18	15	2	-	n/a
I take them to work	3	2	7	-	n/a
I work at home	4	2	0	-	n/a
Old enough to look after themselves	22	29	1	0	n/a
n=	489	262	52	66	289

Formal care indicated in bold.
* indicates where more than half would have to pay for the alternative source.

Parents were also asked what alternative sources they had should their childcare break down. Nine out of ten said their childcare could be relied upon every day or nearly every day, but more than half using any particular source had a back-up. The availability of back-ups gives some indication of how dependent lone parents were on their current source of childcare. Those using their own, older children, unregistered childminders, day nurseries and nursery schools were least likely to have an alternative. There are three possible implications: first, that such sources are chosen more as a last resort, that the parents who use them have few friends or relatives who could step in in an emergency; second, a scarcity of such sources, that duplicate sources could not be found; or, third, that due to larger staff numbers, such sources are less vulnerable to withdrawal. The majority of back-up sources were free – except the back-ups for those parents using day nurseries or crèches, more than half of whom would also have to pay for their alternative. That parents chose to pay for care rather than regularly use their 'free' back-up implies that alternatives could only be drawn upon temporarily, in times of need.

Work on lone parent surveys from 1993 and earlier years calculated that lone parents who paid for childcare paid around one fifth of after-tax earnings in childcare costs (Ford, Marsh and McKay, 1995). The position for the 1994 respondents was much the same. In the absence of an in-work childcare subsidy, therefore, the cost of childcare might be expected to act as a considerable disincentive on lone parents who would have to pay for childcare to enter work.

Holiday care

It is often argued that parents who might take work during school hours are discouraged from working by the potential costs of childcare during school holidays. As few lone parents are able to work only schooldays, the availability and cost of childcare in holidays will be an important consideration.

Among workers, the pattern of use of holiday childcare (Table 2.4) was little different from during term-time (Table 2.3). Some of the term-time contrasts are given additional emphasis: the balance between formal and informal sources, who pays for care and the availability of alternatives. Those using formal sources were even more likely to pay for them and those using holiday play schemes were more dependent on them than those using after-school schemes. Some sources rose in importance during holidays: notably the ex-partner, the children's grandparents and relatives. Among full-time workers, the use of registered childminders was greater than during term-time. The proportions paying for care, and the amounts paid were also slightly higher. Few parents experienced a dramatic increase in costs in moving between term-time and holidays.

Table 2.4   All lone parents who have worked since 1991: childcare in most recent or current job, holiday-time

	All %	All currently working 16+ hrs %	% of those using each form of care who pay/paid for: formal care	informal care	% who have an alternative source
Ex-partner	9	8	3	12	69
Parents (in law)	28	35	3	12	62
Siblings	6	5	5	10	57
Other relatives/friends	21	18	3	41	63
Nursery/crèche	2	2	100	-	68*
Nursery school/playgroup	0	1	100	-	67
Registered childminder	7	6	84	-	62
Unregistered childminder	3	3	-	93	62
Live in nanny/Au pair	1	0	100	-	100
Other daily/shared nanny	0	1	50	-	50
Holiday play scheme	2	2	62	-	43
Non-childcare					
I only work during term-time	7	5	-	-	n/a
I take them to work	3	2	9	-	n/a
I work at home	4	2	0	-	n/a
Old enough to look after themselves	25	29	1	-	n/a
n=	434	262	52	66	289

Formal care indicated in bold.
* indicates where more than half would have to pay for the alternative source

The majority remained with the same sources and paying similar amounts, if paying at all. Of lone parents working 16 or more hours a week in 1994, one-third used no childcare at any time, and three in ten used only free sources throughout the year. Of those who ever paid for care, two-thirds paid in both term-time and holidays. Six per cent shifted from paid term-time to free holiday care. One in six used childcare only during term-time and one in ten used childcare (and paid for it) only during the holidays. In the 1994 survey, only one parent shifted from 'free' term-time care to paid-for care in holidays.

In sum, fewer of those who ever paid for childcare paid only in holidays than paid only during term-time. More than half the ever-payers paid the same during both periods (a mean of £39.70). Nearly a quarter paid more during the holidays (up from £21.20 to £44.40) and 6 per cent paid only during holidays (£32.60 on average), totalling to three in ten those who saw their costs rise during holidays. Fifteen per cent saw their costs fall as they paid only during term-time (£34.40 on average).

While childcare represents a significant in-work cost for those who pay, those who use it generally find it reliable and have alternative sources to call on in an emergency. Only a small number find their childcare costs fluctuating dramatically between term-time and holidays. From data on current workers, therefore, a measured but positive message emerges about how lone parents cope with childcare while working.

Potential childcare use among those out of work

We must take care not to extrapolate these findings from lone parents in work to those who might enter. It may be that those who have access to reliable, relatively cheap or 'free' childcare are more likely to be found in work and thus be among the workers interviewed in 1994. The lack of a substantial differential between term-time and holiday costs may be because those who would encounter such differentials, or could not cope with them financially, absent themselves from the labour market during the most difficult periods, or completely. Similarly, those who experience general difficulties with locating or paying for childcare may be more highly represented among those out of work. Put simply, it could be that those for whom the cost and or availability of childcare does not pose a significant barrier to entry into the labour market are already in work.

To say more about how childcare cost and availability influences lone parents' labour market decisions, we must look also at the preferences and intentions of those out of work. Such data may be more hypothetical in nature, but comparison with the characteristics of those in work should highlight any major differentials between workers and non-workers on the childcare question.

Table 2.5 Childcare out-of-work lone parents would use if they had a job

	Would use %	% would have to pay	% of those with each first choice who have an alternative	Alternative source %
Ex/future partner	5	15	75	6
Parents (in law)	17	41	77	25
Siblings	4	25	75	5
Other relatives/friends	17	69	54	67
Nursery/crèche	**1**	60	55	
Nursery school/playgroup	**2**	100	68	
Registered childminder	**17**	100	40	3
Unregistered childminder	3	100	8	1
Live in nanny/Au pair	**1**	100	11	
After school or holiday play scheme	**1**	58	58	
I would only work during school hours	25	n/a	n/a	3
I would take them to work	0	n/a	n/a	3
I would work at home	0	n/a	n/a	1
Old enough to look after themselves	19	n/a	n/a	2
Don't know	11			
n=	484		142	141

Base: Lone parents not working 16+ hours in 1994 who have sought work in the past 12 months or who 'might look for a paid job one day'.
Formal care indicated in bold.

For example, Table 2.5 presents the sources of childcare out-of-work lone parents said they would use if they were to enter work. As the focus is on potential childcare sources, rather than reasons for staying out of the labour market, the 'out-of-work' definition can be expanded to include again those who have been looking for work. Comparison with Table 2.3 reveals out-of-work lone parents are less likely to call on the childcare services of their parents and are more likely to say they would work only during school hours. Most notably, twice as many anticipate calling on the services of registered or unregistered childminders as is the case among those currently or recently in work. While most out-of-work lone parents see themselves as having alternatives to their hypothetical childcare source, very few of those who would call upon childminders see themselves as having any alternative source of care.

There is thus a significant group among those out of work who can foresee themselves entering work only if they call upon the services of a childminder. The reluctance of others to name childminders as a potential back up source (final column, Table 2.5) suggests that the inclination to use childminders is confined largely to those who do not have access to other sources. However, this should not be taken to imply that childminders are an unpopular source of childcare. When preferences for different sources of childcare are analysed in Chapter 5, we find registered childminders comprise the favoured form of care provision. Only 19 per cent of out-of-work lone parents would never consider using a registered childminder. The pattern of responses in Table 2.5 is more likely to reflect perceived availability and relative cost.

Two-thirds of those not working 16 or more hours who anticipate using some form of childcare once in work of such hours envisage having to pay for it. Virtually all those who anticipate using formal care expect to pay for it. This is a higher proportion than found actually paying among those in work (42 per cent) and suggests that out-of-work lone parents could well perceive a disincentive to enter work because of the cost of childcare.

It is at this point that we reach the conundrum which prompted this study. Although 36 per cent of out-of-work lone parents say childcare costs keep them out of the labour market (Table 2.2), only one third of these parents actually anticipate using a form of childcare in work which would require them to pay. One fifth would use their parents, one in eight would use their relatives or friends and a quarter would use a registered childminder. Among the six in ten who would use some form of childcare, the proportion who expect to pay for it is no higher than among others out of work: two-thirds.

Another third of those who say the cost of childcare keeps them out of work do not anticipate entering work until the need for childcare has subsided. This group comprise the one in ten who do not anticipate entering work until their children are old enough to look after themselves and a quarter who say they would work only school hours. This latter group are no more likely to have children aged under five years than lone parents as a whole (41 per cent versus 39 per cent). Thus one in eight out-of-work lone parents have a youngest child of school age and would work during school hours, but say that it is the cost of childcare which keeps them out of work. Another one in eight do not know what form of childcare they would use in work, but still they say it would cost too much.

Perhaps it is because the anticipated cost of childcare is so high that parents cannot envisage entering work and paying for childcare. Among their alternative strategies may be working only school hours, but the jobs which would allow them to do this without recourse to some childcare are few and far between, hence the apparent anomalies.

So the National Survey has captured some broad differences between in-work and out-of-work lone parents. Workers are more likely to be recruited from the parents of older and fewer children. Many remain out of work because they feel their children are simply too young to spend time apart from their mother. The second most frequently stated reason for not being in work is being unable to afford childcare, but this is stated as often by mothers of five to ten year-olds as mothers of under-fives. However, childcare is just one of a number of barriers on the route back to work, as six in seven who face problems with childcare face at least one other constraint as well.

In the data reviewed so far, lone parents in work appear as a selected group among whom childcare barriers are less commonly encountered. The proportion of lone parents in work who use formal childcare (childminders, in particular) is much smaller than the proportion of out-of-work lone parents who anticipate having to use formal care. Likewise, more out-of-work lone parents than those in work face having to use paid-for childcare.

THE NEED FOR FURTHER RESEARCH

The answers to the National Survey's questions raise other concerns:

- How realistically do lone parents view a return to the labour market?
- How effectively do they weigh up the likely income they will receive in work in terms of earnings, in-work benefit and maintenance?

We have reached the point where analysis of quantitative data is raising as many questions as it answers about how the cost and/or availability of childcare poses a barrier to taking up or remaining in work of 16 or more hours each week. We know that 36 per cent of out-of-work lone parents explicitly identify childcare costs as one factor (and 5 per cent identify cost as the only factor) keeping them out of work of 16 hours or more. But there may be others who do not think specifically in such terms – who say their children are too young or that it is simply not worth working – but who have assimilated problems with childcare into their answers. Others who have placed themselves still further from the labour market – who do not see themselves entering work in the foreseeable future – may have done so because childcare presents an apparently insurmountable problem. Conversely, among those who say childcare cost is the issue are many for whom other labour market problems loom large and who will not be able to enter work before these too are solved. It is also apparent that some are contemplating work from some distance and have not sufficiently addressed the question of which childcare they could use to be able to comment meaningfully on its likely cost.

While cross-sectional quantitative surveys present rigid categorisations of respondents, follow-up surveys can often reveal how flexibly the same people have overcome difficulties. Respondents' characteristics and circumstances differ in ways which may be pertinent to the study question but imperceptible to a pen and paper questionnaire. Thus we may have reached the limits of what a quantitative survey can tell us about how childcare costs and availability intervene in decisions about work. There are simply too many factors which influence the likelihood of lone parents entering work and too many which could act to keep them out of work. While a number of these risk factors will be external, associated with the local labour market and childcare provision, it is how each lone parent's perceptions of such factors interact with their own aims and ambitions that influences their preparedness to work. Unpicking such a complex relationship requires a depth study: one that is reported in the following chapters.

THE DEPTH STUDY

The detail of the Depth Study design appears as Annex A, and the summary topic guide as Annex B. In brief, the aim of the new study was to determine the position occupied by childcare among the labour market barriers of lone parents. In particular it set out to identify those for whom policy initiatives aimed at reducing the cost of childcare will have an effect. 57 interviews were undertaken in early 1995 with lone mothers in three roughly equally-sized groups:

- those known to be out of work or working fewer than 16 hours a week, who had been seeking work in the past 12 months, who had a youngest child aged between 5 and 11 years and who were not pregnant;

- those who had started a job of 16 hours or more each week recently (during 1994), who used childcare and whose youngest was aged under 11 years;

- those who had not sought work of 16 hours or more in the previous 12 months.

The topic guide focused on six dimensions of the work and childcare equation (outlined at Annex A): ability and willingness to take up work; the position of childcare among perceived risks of work entry; the financial incentive to work; views on family separation and childcare preferences; matching vacancies with available childcare, and managing the transition into paid work.

Findings from the Depth Study constitute the majority of the remaining chapters in the report. The chapters follow the order of hypotheses and topic guides in first setting the context in which lone parents differentially affected by the cost and availability of childcare can be identified, before turning to an assessment of the extent of the problems of affordability and availability.

The next chapter draws on material from the earlier stages of each interview which focused on the orientation of each lone mother towards participation in paid work versus spending time at home with her family.

Note

1   Of those who could not foresee a return to work, just under four in ten said illness or disability was keeping them out of the labour market, for example. Only one in 20 felt that there was no childcare available, and one in ten that it cost too much. A third said their children were too young, which suggested that they might contemplate work once their children were older.

Chapter 3

ORIENTATION TO WORK AND FAMILY

This chapter looks at lone mothers' orientations towards their family, their past and current intentions to form and expand their family, towards repartnering and towards fulfilling a home maker role. The interaction between these aims and their orientations to work is explored in this chapter, including their differing financial, career and social motives and how these translate into a motivation to work now or in the future.

The development of a motive to work is tied closely to women's perceptions of their roles in different stages of their lives. Lone parenthood is typically short-lived and accounts for just one stage of the lives of those who experience it. How women see their roles is subject to a range of influences which include upbringing, extent of education, social class and contemporary norms and role models. These determine how likely women are to be motivated to seek work at different stages in their lives. Thus one lone mother may resolve to work only at times when she would in any case be apart from her children: on the weekends when the children stay with their father or during school hours, once they are all at school. Another may resolve to keep her full-time position in the labour market at all costs. A third may see it as her role to keep home until all her children have left home for good. When they had partners, these mothers faced a similar set of choices except that the children's father may have been on hand to provide childcare for longer hours, and indeed the full-time participation rates of lone parents and married mothers differ little. According to the General Household Survey in 1992–4, 16 per cent of lone parents work full-time (30 or more hours each week) compared to 22 per cent of married women with children. Part-time rates differ more substantially, with 23 per cent of lone parents and 42 per cent of mothers in couples working part-time. Among mothers of older children (over five years of age) the difference in full-time participation rates narrows to 23 versus 27 per cent full-time.

Interviewers probed these issues first by tracing the interrelationship of work and family histories since the respondent left school. The discussion focused on how their behaviour matched their aims and opportunities: how far their employment matched their aspirations, and how far their families were planned. Interviews moved on to discuss current and future aims and intentions. A parallel focus was on respondents' interpretations of the attitudes and behaviours of others in their immediate social environment: amongst relatives, friends, neighbours and disseminated from opinion-formers and politicians through the media. Childcare as a specific issue was considered secondary to these aspirations and – unless the respondent raised it as a concern – childcare was not discussed until later in the interviews. It does not feature prominently in respondents' accounts in this chapter.

BECOMING A LONE PARENT

No more than half of Britain's lone parents planned their first pregnancy and most who did had a partner at the time. The proportion declines to one in six among those who did not have a partner living with them at the time (Marsh, Ford and Finlayson, 1996 forthcoming). Such a statistic could be taken as evidence that family formation did not feature highly among half these women's aims when they became parents. Carrying this logic through would suggest never-partnered parents to be the least family-orientated when they conceived. If parents orientated to family are less orientated to work, then the low-level of family planning might suggest high work motivation among lone parents. Yet such conclusions do not concur with what is known of lone parents' labour market participation: the never-partnered are the least likely to be economically active, and those who planned their families within marriage are the most likely to have full-time work.

It is also unsafe to assume work and family orientations are opposing ends of a spectrum of motivation: parents can be strongly orientated to both, or to neither. Neither motivation may correspond to their behaviour. Women may want a family and a job, but have neither. Those with work but no children might have preferred to raise children at home, and vice versa. But if we can gain a picture of how becoming a parent and becoming a lone parent interacts with parents' orientation to work, then we should move a step nearer to seeing what aims lone parents are achieving in their current position. We should also discover whether parents would be moving closer or further away from these aims by moving into work. In other words, to the extent to which parents' past family orientations inform their current stance, we can determine the scope of the role that paid work could play in their lives in the future without compromising those aims.

Discussions about family formation touch on sensitive and personal areas of people's lives – particularly so where the discussants are lone parents. Probing the issue of long-term family planning among those who entered parenthood when young, and in the context of insensitive media portrayals of 'welfare mums', is a difficult task. Parents will present only some of the picture and it is important that imagination or prejudice does not supply the rest.

Work orientation and family orientation are not subjects amenable to direct questions. A picture of respondents' life aspirations, opportunities and constraints is built up from their discussions on a wide range of topics, from their first experiences with work and with starting a family, from their plans on leaving school, and how these evolved with the arrival of partners and children, and with the breakdown of relationships.

Lone parents with no real work experience are not common; between 5 and 10 per cent have never had jobs. So all respondents had spent at least some time economically active, looking for work or actually in work. Typically they were most active once they left school, and entered the world of employment before the world of partnerships and child-rearing.

BECOMING A WORKER

Work orientation covers a wide range of motives from seeking short-term financial gain to long-term career motives featuring postponement of early gain for more substantial later income security. Women may show a strong motivation to work, but feel constrained by their immediate circumstances or job opportunities. On the other hand, an individual may not have formulated life plans, but see work as the most immediate way of satisfying immediate needs. Entering employment may simply be the most conspicuous inclination among a set of not very strongly held aspirations. Thus any aims the woman has towards work, and her economic activity at any one time may not coincide. The benefits of work and of different types of worker-role may be perceived differently as time proceeds, while the overall motivation to work remains high. Alternatively, a deterioration in satisfaction with the returns from work when it offers only short-term gains may decrease work motivation.

Few lone parents are highly qualified and most left school at 16 years or earlier. Sampling procedures made no attempt to exclude well-educated lone mothers, but not one of the 60 selected had a degree, and few had gone on to 'A' levels. To the extent that they held any aspirations or plans for how life would unfold when they left school, the focus of even the earliest school-leavers was on becoming workers rather than mothers:

Joanna, 33, left school at 15, having taken no exams, for a full-time job as a supermarket cashier. A direction which she looked back on with disapproval.

I just wanted to get out of school, live in this big world and earn money. I was stupid.

Although not adverse to having children, she would have preferred them later. She became pregnant while working in her second job as a hotel receptionist and never returned to full-time work. Similarly, Susan, now 41, had no ideas about what she would do when she left school, except to start work.

I just wanted to make some money.

It is difficult to ascribe to Joanna or Susan any long-term aspirations when they started employment. They had a short-term aim which work fulfilled but neither entered work which they perceived as rewarding or full of prospects. This lack of direction led less to a disillusionment with the world of work, but frustration and disappointment with the opportunities their routes into employment had denied them.

They had chosen work which solved immediate financial problems for themselves and which relieved their dependence on their families. Other courses of action – such as seeking training for more highly skilled work – might have carried higher risks, particularly if the investment had not paid off. It is difficult for women leaving school who come from families without substantial financial resources to gain support for such risk-taking. One hypothesis is that on leaving school these women take work which offers the maximum short-term gains because their families lack the resources to support them through more risky strategies.

Another divorcee, May, 35 and a mother of two, gave up a promising job with career prospects in a department store to work for her stepfather in a soft toy factory, as it turned out, for nine years.

> *I gave it up voluntarily. I think I was just too young to decide what I wanted to do, to be perfectly honest. I mean, I didn't want to work in a factory, either, I just sort of got stuck with that ... it's often the devil you know is easiest.*

Although she learned interlocking – a transferable skill – the short-term gains of working in a family business were soon outstripped by the perceived losses of having given up a fast-track career. She now spends a few hours each week as an insurance collector.

Other women had better job prospects which they had built up through staying on in school or training. These women spoke very positively about their work and their belief in what it offered their lives, both financially and in terms of the self-fulfilment that comes from greater responsibility. Some had persisted with these careers through to the present day. Others had to accommodate the career aims of their partners, or had to adapt following the arrival of children. The drawback of specialising in skilled occupations was a lack of flexibility over the hours worked and the number of potential jobs available, so matching work and family responsibilities was made more difficult.

In a sense such 'career' women had conflicting aims, their life plans were built jointly around their own work and their relationship with a partner. Conflicts arose when the needs of one role intervened in another. Sadie, 34, was a local authority worker whose career progression was damaged when she had to move to satisfy her husband's job mobility.

I've always wanted to get on in my job, and I think if I'd stayed in [home town] I would have done a lot better. I mean, I always had to go back to the beginning when we moved with my husband's job. Moved to [next location], I had to go back to the beginning then. Moved back to [home town], back to the beginning again. He might have thought he was getting on, but I felt as if I was going down all the time.

When her husband started to have affairs, Sadie left him. In the context of a relationship, providing support for his career advancement at the expense of her own may have seemed an acceptable trade-off. In the context of lone parenthood, it seemed short-sighted. After the separation, she was able to stay in her home town, but her career prospects had already been severely damaged. At the time of interview she had been able to match her skills only to a poorly-paid part-time post. She had been holding out in the expectation of full-time work or a promotion, but was becoming increasingly demoralised and underpaid, and had reached the position where she was considering entering unskilled occupations which would reduce her work responsibilities at little (short-term) financial cost.

I don't see any harm in part-time work. I know people argue it's low paid. It's maybe not the best job, like cleaning and different things, which I wouldn't really want to do, to be honest. But I actually did think about it when I wasn't getting on anywhere in my job. 'Well, do a cleaning job: no responsibility; come out; forget about it.' I mean that's actually the stage I was getting to.

A handful of others had kept well-paid careers going since they left education. They had not relinquished their professional or managerial jobs upon entry into relationships, parenthood or lone parenthood. Although they reported difficulties, and occasional spells out of work (one on Income Support), the work motivation had remained strong throughout their lives. Ruth and Shirley who had given up careers when they married, regretted it now that they felt unable to return (see below).

This is perhaps the clearest finding from discussions of work histories: that women who had always being strongly motivated to work, remained so through their marriages, through parenthood and now into lone parenthood. The constraints on their ability to remain in employment varied with each stage, but regardless of economic status at any one time, they continued to think of themselves as workers.

A strong belief in economic activity did not necessarily translate into participation in full-time work. Elizabeth, a 29 year-old divorced mother of two, aged seven and eight, believed her five hours of pub work each week sufficient to meet the obligations she felt.

> *I've always worked, I mean I've always done a bit of work, it might not have been a lot, but I've always tried. I don't think anybody should be entitled to just sit back and let the State keep them.*

Lone mothers were asked directly what effect becoming a lone parent had on their intentions to work. Sue, 29, had continued her career in secretarial and administrative work into lone parenthood. She felt her underlying ambitions were altered little by her separation and divorce.

> *At that time I suppose it didn't actually change my ideas, I had quite strong ideas about what I wanted to do anyway. I knew I wanted to go out to work and I had to go back to work, so it was a question of making the best of it really.*

And Alison, a never-partnered mother who had recently worked as a cook now as a sewing machinist, held similar views. Throughout the interview, she equated her 'life' with going out to work and separate from her responsibilities for her one year-old daughter. Even so, she checked herself from saying that work was something she actually enjoyed.

> *As soon as I knew I was pregnant, I'd made the decision that I'd go back to work. I know we haven't got much money now, but I thought – especially with the money – if I don't go to work, we're going to have even less money. And I like, not like, going to work, but I didn't want my life to stop, just 'cos I had [my daughter].*

Thus lone parents with an orientation to work differed in their success in the labour market according to the constraints posed by financial pressures when they were younger, the skills they were able to acquire and the need to combine their career roles with responsibilities towards their family and partners.

Although the women interviewed had all had contact with the labour market, there were many – around half those found out of work at the time of interview – for whom the attachment had from the outset been secondary to other goals. Most of these women had set out to follow more traditional family roles, and although this did not rule out contact with the labour market, it was not centre stage.

TRADITIONAL ROLE

The 'traditional' family structure of a male breadwinner and female homemaker, mother and wife represents a minority of modern families. Most married women work, and many families comprise unmarried couples and lone parents. It is less certain for whom a traditional model still represents an aspiration or ideal that circumstances have failed to allow, or for whom among the members of traditional families the arrangement represents an achieved goal. In 1989, a survey of social attitudes found women almost equally divided on attitude items such as 'a job is all right, but what most women really want is a home and children' and more than four in ten agreed that 'a husband's job is to earn money; a wife's job is to look after the home and family' (Scott and Duncombe, 1991).

Respondents do not have to occupy a traditional role to aspire to it. A former full-time worker, Emma, 39, had entered parenthood unexpectedly and spent time in an unmarried mother's home.

> *I'd have been quite happy to be married and my husband bringing in a good wage and me staying at home with the kids. I would have been perfectly happy with that.*

She did marry, following the arrival of her second child – incidentally conforming to a trend towards the separation of childbirth and marriage identified by Marsh, Ford and Finlayson (1996 forthcoming). Entry into marriage permitted her departure from employment, about which she expressed few regrets.

I just worked in [factory] after that, I think for four years and then [second child] was born so that was me. I got married then and that's been me since. I've not worked since ... that was me: I stayed at home.

Emma was able to pursue her family aspirations but her husband drank heavily and argued which she found financially and emotionally draining and which precipitated their separation. She had not worked since 1979. Thus as a working parent, Emma had aspired to financial support through marriage and a traditional child-rearing role. Her work motivation was sufficiently weak for her to cease employment as soon as the financial necessity of work diminished.

Such aspirations can be modelled on the parental home. Lone parents frequently looked to their own upbringing for examples of child rearing. They may share this characteristic with other parents, or may find themselves doing so more in the absence of a partner with whom to establish a model of how children should be brought up.

Although she had worked one morning a week as a hairdressing assistant, Janine, 29, was out of work at the time of interview. She recognised that her strong desire to remain at home with the children was distinct from her lack of enthusiasm for what the labour market could offer, and was different from the views of other women. Her own upbringing, non-traditional in many ways after her own mother had left her family, informed Janine's decision to stay with her own two children full-time.

I mean, it's not, 'I want to be with my children', just out of sake of not wanting to go to work. You want to be with that child because you love that child, and I suppose a lot of mothers don't feel it. I feel as if my dad was there for me, and I'm there for my kids. My dad wouldn't bung me off to school, and then 'That's it, I'm going back to work'. He gave us the best years of his life.

For a never-partnered mother, once the decision to have or keep a child has been made, the mother has committed herself to a new set of responsibilities which require a different division of activities between home and work. Jess, 29, had a long and committed history of full-time work in driving occupations before she became pregnant. Although she still planned to return to work, and lived with her own mother, she felt that her first duty was to be available for her two year-old son.

> *I could never go back to the lorries because I would want to [work] between the hours that [my son] goes to school ... If you're going to be a parent, you might as well be there for him*

But while a work role can last forty or more years, the most intense demands of parenting are concentrated into half that time or less. Thus even a traditional combination of wife, home-making and child-rearing roles must come to an end. The child-rearer role will become less involved as children grow older. Lone parents are already denied the role of wife and, once children are at school, spend increasing periods when the sole occupation for an out-of-work lone mother is that of homemaker.

> *They're not babies any more. I don't need to be there sort of 24 hours. They don't need me 'cos they're at school now as well. And I've just come to part of my life, I think: 'What am I doing? I'm not going nowhere, I'm not doing anything', and I think now I've got to do something for the three of us.* [Joanna]

Lone mothers frequently give voice to expressions of boredom and frustration with their role. The extent to which such feelings provide a motive for a return to work is discussed below. Child-rearing as an occupation is short lived, and as Joanna alludes 'doing the best for one's children' can require financial resources unavailable to the out-of-work lone mother. The traditional role might then be most logically pursued by finding a new, employed partner. But lone parents have reason to doubt the efficacy of such a route, and may also acknowledge the difficulty of locating a partner, employed or otherwise, while they are out of work and when the only free time they have is during school hours. Repartnering is discussed further below.

Some parents explicitly recognised that, in child-rearing, they themselves were setting examples for their children. Securing earned income might thus form part of the 'child-rearing' role, regardless of orientation to work, as Sarah, a part-time worker on Family Credit, acknowledged.

My aim in life is to do, obviously, the best for the children. I didn't want them to suffer financially, or emotionally. And I felt that I was getting fed up with being at home. I wanted to go out to work to give them a role model. I wanted them to think that Mum was there, at home, doing the home. But I also wanted them to think that there was a breadwinner in the family.

This view was echoed by Elaine, while Sally, 33, a personal assistant, stressed the fine line between meeting her responsibilities and aspirations for her children with those she had for herself.

I've got to provide them with a good home and let them do all the things that all the other children at their school do. So it's just the line you have to draw. I have to work full-time and that's it. I mean if I had my choice I'd be at home with them all the time.

Thus a traditional role which encompassed being a child-rearer, a homemaker and a wife still held sway for a number of lone parents, regardless of their contact with the labour market. But the existence of such aspirations did not – of itself – prevent such parents reaching a stage of parenthood where working became an option again. However, these aspirations did mean that in planning to work, such parents were putting their perception of their children's interests first. They were very unlikely to be found in full-time work, for example.

ACCEPTING PARENTAL RESPONSIBILITIES

In discussing orientation towards child-rearing, it is important not to overlook women for whom events overtook the fulfilment of any aspirations to work or to family. While the majority of lone parents have their first child within marriage, and around half plan when to start their families, some are lone parents before any other life roles intervene. Not only have such parents short-circuited any goals or aims they might have had, they have very little experience of what different life roles might offer.

It is worth considering here decisions made to start or keep a family, since the outcome of these decisions has long-term consequences for job prospects and also reflects on lone mothers' perceptions of their life roles.

Unexpected teenage pregnancy need not always lead to lone parenthood. Pregnant women may opt for abortion or offer up the child for adoption. Since the 1970s there has been a decline in the incidence of abortion as an outcome for teenage pregnancies (Coleman and Salt, 1993), and certainly few of the teenage mothers in our sample talked of abortion as an option. Only one mother had postponed parenthood by giving up her first-born child for adoption.

At the age of 16, Susan gave up her baby for adoption, some ten days after the birth. She was one of the older respondents and attributed her decision in part to the moral climate of the time and in part to financial necessity.

> *It was like growing up in about ten minutes flat ... and there was no money, it wasn't like now, I couldn't just have gone on benefit ... I didn't regret that decision, I think at the time it was the best thing to do.*

Among the small number who openly discussed abortion was Meg, 23. The child's father, whom she never lived with, was subsequently killed in an accident.

> *I did think about getting rid of her, but I wouldn't have done it ... It was really weird because one minute I was a wild teenager, the next minute I had a lot of responsibility. It was just as though it had been chucked on your shoulders.*

To consider abortion, Meg, or whoever was advising her, was recognising that she might not have been ready to take on the role and responsibilities of child-rearing. Interviewers were not asked to probe the reasons, which could be emotional, financial or defined by a moral or religious code, but there is a recognition that bringing a child into a family where the woman has not yet formed her long term goals and aspirations could be detrimental.

Another never-partnered mother found that becoming pregnant and deciding to keep the child disrupted her relationship with the child's father whose aims did not match her own. In declining abortion she forsook her ambitions for a partnership.

I decided to have [my son], and then things went really sour. Basically. And I hadn't got the courage to do what a lot of mothers do, to get out of the situation. [Janine]

Deliberate lone parenthood is very rare (Ford, Marsh and McKay, 1995). Even those strongly orientated towards starting and raising a family rarely do so before some time has been spent in work and in a relationship. Thus very few parents make deliberate decisions to have their children when young. Only one respondent had chosen to have her children when a teenager. Elaine spoke of a deliberate strategy to leave the rest of her life 'free' for other things. She juxtaposes child-rearing with things she wants to do. She was training to become a mortgage adviser – work which she hoped would pay her through nursing college. She spoke almost as if child-rearing were compulsory, such that she has chosen to pursue it early to get it over with.

It was planned, because I would have rather had them, to get it all over and done with ... and then I can sort of start again now, whereas if I'd have wanted any more it would have dragged on a lot longer. It would have been a lot longer time before I could have done anything I wanted to do.

These never-partnered parents entered parenthood and lone parenthood at the same time. While it is not fair to say that Janine chose lone parenthood, both she and Elaine were aware that from the outset they would be taking on sole responsibility for the child's upbringing. Any decisions made about the necessity of combining a work role with parenthood would be their own from the start. The majority of lone mothers, who separate from their children's father, could have undertaken to have children in very different circumstances from those in which they found themselves bringing them up.

For these women, the transition to lone parenthood can be a traumatic one. Nearly all couples argue during the year before separation, four in ten come to blows and more than a quarter of the women who become lone parents report physical injury (Marsh, Ford and Finlayson, 1996 forthcoming). At the time of separation, disputes are likely over the division of belongings and the custody of children. These events in themselves could be expected to interfere with, or supplant, the mother's motivation to work.

Separation, divorce and widowhood all rate highly as stressful life events (Furnham and Bochner, 1986). Evidence suggests that on entering lone parenthood, mothers face considerable emotional challenges: supporting children, reorganising household affairs, often moving house (Leeming, Unell and Walker, 1994).

One mother who had taken time to adjust was Marion, 36, who suffered chronic obstructive airways disease and had a history of family tragedy. She lost her son in a house fire and had undertaken a long-distance council house exchange to escape a subsequent partner who attacked her and abused her children. She had worked as a chambermaid until she suffered a blood clot on her lung. She was just beginning to seek work again at the time of the interview.

Since lone parent families have almost by definition experienced disruptive events and transitions, at any one time a proportion must be expected to be spending time out of work engaged in readjusting their families' lives to the changed circumstances.

Since few set out to enter lone parenthood, few can be fully prepared for the challenges it poses. They will take some time to adapt. If they were working prior to entry, they may need to stop work to see to the immediate needs of their home and their family. If they were not working, it seems unlikely that getting a new job will be their highest priority.

A third of lone parents left their partner's household upon separation. Accounts speak of the urgency of the departure, moving in temporarily with friends or family, and longer-term dilemmas deciding the family's new location and housing. Those who had to organise the children's departure while attempting to maintain continuity in their schooling found it difficult to maintain full-time hours through the separation. Even those whose partners left faced difficulties reorganising their lives. Women who had built their world around caring for children as part of a partnership, like Marie, a mother of three, spoke of the time it took to adjust to lone parenthood.

I think that's the worst of it. It does take a long time to get used to being on your own, and being able to cope with children on your own.

Any survey of lone parents is likely to pick up more who have been so for a long time. Those who leave lone parenthood quickly, because they reconcile with their former partner or find a new one, are less likely to be part of a cross-section sample. Thus most of the lone parents interviewed here had been so for some years, and had adjusted to life without a partner. In doing so, they had made opportunities to leave lone parenthood through repartnering seem less attractive.

Ruth was a 35 year-old, divorced mother of nine and eight year-old children. She had worked full-time when married in various jobs, including as a bank cashier and receptionist.

> *I'm seeing someone and you never know, but I think I like my independence a little bit. I know that I'm skint but at least I've got my independence ... Possibly in a few years, maybe. It's frightening after you've sort of made a big cock up once. You're frightened of doing it again.*

Being strongly family orientated may prolong lone parenthood if it results in a desire for more children. Regardless of whether or not the lone mother repartners, having more children has been found independently to lengthen the amount of time spent out of work (Ford, Marsh and Finlayson, 1996 forthcoming).

Having a larger family was clearly part of Sadie's life plans which she was reluctant to give up. Nonetheless she felt guilty about her wishes to have more children while she was still a lone mother.

> *That's the bad thing. I would like to have children ... I'm what, 35 next year, but I don't really see it. I think if I don't, I'll be quite upset about it. I'd also like someone for [my daughter].*

Parents might persist with family building, taking their own family as role model.

> *My mum's got four and, I mean, she seems to be coping alright with it.* [Meg]

More common among those who wished for more children was a recognition that lone parenthood did not provide the ideal context for child rearing. Circumstances would have to change before an addition to the family could be contemplated.

*I shouldn't imagine I would have any more, in reality, but in my
dreams it would be nice to have one ... It's something I would consider if I met a chap and we settled down, I got married again and
circumstances and finances said 'Yes, I could have another one',
then I would. But in reality I can't see it happening. I'm 33 now so
haven't got that long in which to do all of that. I can't see it. Settle
for the two.* [Sally]

For some, of course, the decision to have children could not be
separated from the context of the earlier partnership. In the
absence of the partnership, the orientation to family was weak-
ened. Eileen was a 27 year-old mother of a one year-old, separated
from cohabitation.

*I've always dreamt of having loads of children. Anyway I couldn't.
I couldn't afford it. I wouldn't like them all to have different dads.*

And Mary, a 31 year-old agoraphobic mother of an eight year-old,
for whom having children made little sense without her ex-
partner.

I'm not childminded.

Of course, lone mothers' caring responsibilities did not always end
with their children. Seven per cent of lone parents in the 1994
National Survey cared for someone else who was ill. For four out
of five of these lone parents, this person lived outside their home.
In sum, some 15 per cent of lone parents felt constrained from
working by their need to care for an ill child or other ill person, or
by their own illness. Janine cared for her disabled father.

*My world does revolve round my dad. I mean, it wouldn't be nor-
mal if I didn't go to my dad's.*

There are thus many reasons why mothers with even a high work
motivation may spend time out of the labour market. They may
have children unexpectedly or deliberately, suffer the breakdown
of a relationship around which their work role had been structured, and simply find the pressures of solo parenthood – or at
least adjustment to it – too overwhelming to pursue a career at the
same time.

Among lone parents are also many who structured their lives around a traditional triad of roles: as wife, mother and homemaker. These parents did not see anything but a temporary role for work in achieving their life's ambitions. But they lost their first role with separation, and the importance of the second diminishes as their children age. These parents might find themselves increasingly dissatisfied with their sole remaining role. Still others may see breadwinning as a family function they are prepared to pursue *in the absence* of anyone else. Yet others may find that simply to fulfil child-rearing and homemaking roles to their satisfaction they require an income which exceeds that available on benefits.

WORKING THROUGH FINANCIAL NECESSITY

This is not a forum in which to discuss the material deprivation and low incomes of lone parent families. It is sufficient to reiterate findings from elsewhere (Marsh and McKay, 1993b) that as a group they survive on lower incomes and suffer greater material hardship than most low-income couple families, and most other types of household.

Financial security was discussed in interviews to determine how parents' subjective evaluations of their circumstances translated into a desire to seek higher incomes, and if so how they sought to do so. It was such a pervasive concern for those in hardship that financial needs were discussed in many other contexts as well.

There was little doubt in these parents' minds that their families' low income was one of the major problems they faced. Maureen, 31, was the divorced mother of an eight year-old. She was a trained psychiatric nurse now doing unpaid voluntary work within school hours. She discussed her ever-pressing financial circumstances in the context of having more children. She felt that the lack of finances affected the material and emotional quality of her child-rearing.

I wouldn't want to have another child and bring her up the way [my daughter has] been brought up so far. It's just 'can't have'. Her friends have and she can't have, and I must always be moaning about money. I don't mean to moan at her all the time. But most of our conversations must revolve around money, and the fact that I haven't got any. We'll go out to the shops and she'll say 'Can I

*have a lucky bag?' It's 50 pence. And I'll say [shouts] 'I've no
money!' and that's really not her fault, but it's just awful, and it's
no way to have another child, being brought up in those circumstances.*

Lone mothers who are not orientated towards work themselves
should nonetheless have a strong incentive to take a job if it will
change their circumstances: it will improve the quality of other
aspects of their lives and bring them closer to achieving other
goals. Even those without a strong work motivation see the major
route to better material circumstances through the labour market.

Rachel, 29, separated from a cohabitation, had worked in the
clothing trade and as a homeworker. She had a two year-old and a
seven year-old daughter.

*I'd like a bit of me own independence back – which I've lost. You
know, it would just be nice. And to have a bit of extra money in
your pocket, as well. It's terrible, when you have to penny-pinch,
all the time, and your money's accounted for.*

Where financial necessity provides the major reason for work
entry, the decision to remain in work will be based on the balance
of financial gains to other (financial and non-financial) losses. It
was two years after the birth of the first of her three children that
Jane, now 28, had to return to work, shelving. She did so because
her husband had stopped working.

*I think he'd either stopped work or was off sick for a while, or
something like that, you know and we needed the money.*

But over time, the late hours of the shelving job meant Jane had an
unpleasant and potentially risky journey home, catching the last
bus of the day on two routes. The financial recompense was not
sufficient and she left the job.

So financial necessity as a motive works both ways. If the gain
from work is not sufficient, the parent may leave employment.
Ruth left work because, as a mortgage payer, she could not meet
her housing costs in work. Her husband was not prepared to leave
the house if he remained financially liable for the mortgage. Only
by leaving work and claiming Income Support could she get her
husband to leave.

> *So the only way I could get him out of the house was for him to*
> *not have to fork out financially, so that the only way I could do it*
> *was go on Income Support: they pay the interest on the mortgage.*

Similarly, because both Janine's children were ill, she could not keep up her part-time job. At the same time, she did not appear reluctant to let the job go.

> *I think it was three Wednesdays running that I couldn't get in … I*
> *says, 'I'm going to have to let you down again', I says, 'and I won't*
> *be put out if you've got to find someone else, to fill me in'. And she*
> *said 'OK then' and I noticed she'd got someone else working*
> *Wednesdays.*

We return to the issue of incentives in the next chapter. It is sufficient to conclude here that when money is the sole motive for work, lone parents are quick to see its disadvantages and the advantages of not working.

WORKING AS A CHANGE OF ROUTINE

Undoubtedly, many respondents were in severe financial difficulties, and a number were in severe material hardship according to the index devised by Marsh and McKay (1993b). In this context, lone mothers talked of the financial benefits of taking up work. However, the most consistent theme among out-of-work mothers was not the financial rewards from work, but how it would relieve their boredom. Many viewed their time at home as unrewarding and empty: work offered more opportunities to leave behind the monotony of home life than it did for financial improvement. This may reflect a realistic assessment of the likely net financial returns from work, or simply that out-of-work lone mothers value social rewards more highly than economic ones. Those who valued financial gains might be more often found among those with a strong orientation to work, or among those with better-paid jobs.

Jenny, 26, was a never-partnered mother of a four year-old who had been laid off from full-time work at a cash and carry.

I'd rather work than be sat idle doing nothing. I'd rather be doing something, you know what I mean? I'm sat like the Life of Riley at the moment, I don't like it. I'd rather be doing something.

Eileen returned to work between births. Her first child had chosen to live with his father. She described what the job meant to her.

It was something to fill the time in, with not having [first child] any more. It was something to do really.

A variation on this theme was voiced by Claire, 30, a Family Credit claimant and mother of three separated from marriage, who spoke of the positive effects of work on her mental health.

It's not really the money. Though it does help and it makes the world go round, doesn't it, but with me it keeps my sanity going.

Parents varied in the extent to which the financial gains paralleled the social and emotional release the change of environment offered. Cathy, 23, was a never-partnered mother of two children aged seven and two years. She worked 29 hours each week as a barmaid and claimed Family Credit.

It's a break off the kids: money, mostly money. It's time to get away from the kids for a wee while, definitely. Sometimes I go insane 'cos it's my day off. I thought: 'How could I cope?'

The need for adult company and stimulation offered by most sorts of work was very highly valued by all who spoke of it. Some lone parents felt isolated because of their geographic location, and others felt socially isolated by their status. More commonly though, it was the absence of another adult in the home which encouraged the lone mother into employment. Likewise, parents spoke of the tedium posed by the constant company of young children.

Tracy, 38, worked as a temporary secretary. She had two daughters, now aged ten and six.

When you've got a husband that's never there and you're stuck at home all day. She was only four at the time. And you need something more, so I decided to go back.

Maxine, 22, also separated from marriage, had a one year-old and a three year-old. She had work experience spanning typing, waitressing, shop and market work and sandwich-making.

> *Everywhere you go, you've got to have two kids around.*

One way open to lone parents to engage new adult company without the responsibility or financial uncertainties of paid work was to take up voluntary work. Only two spent considerable parts of their day in such activities, however, and both were looking increasingly to enter better-paid full-time work. Maureen was one.

> *I'd like to go back to work. I'm really getting fed up. I mean I work voluntary, but you know I'd like to be paid for what I do.*

Jobs undertaken principally to relieve boredom were seldom full-time, however, and often the simplest of jobs would suffice. Claire spoke of the benefits of her work as a bus station cleaner.

> *It's something else I can talk about as well, besides the family. It was very boring: 'What did you do today?' 'Well, I put me daughter on the toilet' or 'I decorated'. I'm too young for that. I'm only a baby myself. There's more to life than talking about a house.*

Non-workers like Josie, 22, who lived in her parents' house with her brothers and her four year-old daughter, described the tedium of the school day.

> *I'm bored through the day. 'Cos I've got nothing to do. It's either like sitting here or sitting in other people's houses drinking cups of tea and it's really depressing and miserable.*

These many accounts present very similar rationales for seeking part-time work, largely during school hours. Work was not viewed as a solution to financial problems, but equally, few spoke of the financial disincentives of work entry. They were not saying the financial incentive to enter work was sufficient in itself to encourage entry, but the social benefits of getting out of the home and altering the daily routine could make work worthwhile. This is important because although an underlying motivation to work was not in evidence for such mothers, the chances of them entering at least part-time work seemed fairly high, provided the work was available and it did not interfere with their other commitments. If the reason for going out to work was because staying at home was becoming frustrating, they were unlikely to swap home life for a stressful job.

Less obvious in these accounts is evidence of a long-term life goal. Employment is seen as a solution to problems which have recently arisen as children place fewer demands on their parents. This does not appear to be a problem that they foresaw when their children were younger and more demanding. Nowhere in these accounts do parents speak of how their work might develop or what they might be doing in ten years' time, when their children leave home. The horizons of these mothers are short-term and it is the immediate rather than long-term gains and losses arising from parenthood and employment that are being compared.

Maria, 21, mother of a one year-old, had trained as a hair-dresser before her pregnancy. She had subsequently separated from her husband. The prospect of time without her daughter present had turned her thoughts to work.

> No, I wasn't looking for a job, but now [my daughter]'s getting older and I'm thinking 'I could get out'. And the debt what I'm in and everything. Now she's coming up to nursery it's made me think. Perhaps I can get a part-time job … Sometimes I think, if I could get a job and get out it'd give us both a break. 'Cos she could benefit from seeing somebody else as well.

The potential for work entry among lone parents is thus substantially enlarged when children become old enough to enter day-care and school. The financial benefits of doing so were subservient to the social gains the parents saw in a change of routine and expanding their range of adult contact. It was these short-term gains that parents focused on, and the types of work sought were thus largely part-time and during school hours.

COMMITMENT TO WORK

A motivation to participate in work, part-time or full-time, emerges from these accounts as a vital component of a successful transition into employment and retention in work. It is, however, no guarantee that the lone parent will be able to find work of the kind she feels appropriate to her family's needs and circumstances. For example, in common with women in couples, many expressed a preference for part-time work during school hours. But vacancies which fit this 'ideal' model of part-time work are few, especially when the requirement for time off during school holidays is added. Typically such jobs are limited to those in the education system itself.

Thus in many instances, a very strong orientation towards work was thwarted by the availability of work to match school hours. Parents took up posts they found less suitable or with hours they liked less and which failed to match their hopes.

Sadie was highly motivated, but could not find a full-time job to match her skills. So she made do with a part-time post. As seen above, the lack of a sufficient reward from this post had damaged Sadie's motivation to seek more demanding roles, and she was contemplating deskilling herself.

> *I couldn't get anything full time, so rather than have nothing, I took job-share as in part-time ... I got a letter yesterday saying I'd got a permanent post but at the bottom of the scale, so I'm back to doing what I was doing 16 years ago, just for the sake of having a job.*

This disillusionment could lead to lone parents questioning their own orientation to work. When contemplating why she was in work, Alison talked about her continuation in work in terms more commonly heard from benefit claimants discussing their dependence on Income Support.

> *I sometimes think to myself I should ask myself that question. But it's just an on-going thing, isn't it? It's hard to get out of work if you've started. I mean, I can't see me just going down to Income Support, and say, 'I want to go on Income Support'. You've got to have reasons. Stuck in a rut, I suppose.*

There is a fine line between the effect poor rewards from work have on motivation, and the incentives debate discussed in the next chapter. The distinction is made by the unwillingness of the highly motivated to consider a financial argument for reverting to life out of work on Income Support. Sadie and Alison are both Family Credit claimants and do not question whether they are better off financially in work. Their disaffection is because the rewards from work that shaped their positive orientation towards employment are not realised in the jobs they have been able to get.

Steph, 32, was a divorcee who lived with her parents and her six year-old daughter. Even when she mentions her low salary, she is not trying to rationalise whether or not it pays her to work compared to life on benefits. It is her disappointment that the skills she has built up through training to become a legal secretary have not been recognised.

> *They basically offered me £5,000 a year. If it's not junior's salary, it's basically part-time money, on full-time hours. And because I was quite desperate, I decided to take the job, anyway. I just want to go back to work really.*

Sue, also dissatisfied, refused to contemplate life out of work.

> *I can't give up work, I can't think like that. If I give up work what do I do, because I've got no other finances.*

Work fulfilled many roles besides financial support. The structure and discipline of the working day in a high street store offered Janet, a 38 year-old divorced mother of a 9 and a 12-year old, a clear role at a time when alternatives were under threat.

> *I was very run down. If I hadn't got a job I wouldn't have got out of bed in the morning. You know, I was very low at that stage. We'd just split up.*

These 'career' women are strongly committed to work – it is one of their life roles. They seem unlikely to leave employment because they cannot see their lives structured in another way. But what of those whose principal reason for seeking work is for financial gain? The incentives issue should loom larger for lone parents out of work who contemplate returning for reasons of financial necessity. It does, as the next chapter demonstrates, but there are other problems too. Lone parents with a strong family orientation but who want to augment that role with additional cash can find it difficult to visualise fitting their full-time child-rearing and homemaking roles into the time left free either side of a full-time job. For example, June, 22, had worked as a petrol station manager but now could not square employment with her domestic responsibilities: her three year-old son and new baby.

> *I've thought about it so many times, going back to work. I mean, until you actually sit and think about it, you don't realise, you think, 'Oh, I can just go back to work, there'll be no problem'. But you can't. You've got to think of who's going to look after the children. Who's going to feed them? Who's going to shop for me, and obviously, if I was working full-time, I wouldn't have time to go shopping. The shopping's got to be done in the week. That's a different thing, the thought of somebody else practically bringing your children up. And when the children get sick, I mean, if they ever got sick, I wouldn't be able to leave them with a childminder, I'd want to be there myself.*

Joanna talked about work almost as if it was a punishment that society was trying to impose on her for being a lone parent. She saw orientation to work and to family as polar opposites.

> *It's not always the mother's fault that she's on her own, and she's the one that's caring for the children and sort of supporting them, loving them and bringing them up, and to go out to work, you've got to give that up, and I don't think it's fair on the children.*

And Sarah, a Family Credit claimant, translated this role conflict into day-to-day time budgeting.

> *Sometimes, I feel that housework, and job, and children: there aren't enough hours in the day. I can't keep on top. I mean, I try. I'm quite house-proud ... That's why I would never, ever, work full-time. Not while I'm on my own.*

Jackie, 38, was separated from marriage and living with her partially deaf 14 year-old son. She held a similar view to Sarah when asked for her views on whether women with pre-school children should work full-time. Though she had worked for seven years full-time while she brought up her children, she attributed this to financial necessity and regretted it with hindsight.

> *I know I did it but I do regret doing it.*

June and Sarah are caught between two stools, they cannot find space for a full-time work role alongside their other roles. If they work, it will only be a part-time job, which is unlikely to provide the financial gains which prompted their consideration of returning to work in the first place. Sarah has been able to secure part-time wages which she can supplement with Family Credit. As such, she can just keep up with each of her roles, but she seems unlikely to move up to more hours in the near future.

Many parents could not imagine this equilibrium position that Sarah had found. They felt that for the income from paid work to make a difference, the work would have to be full-time and thus incompatible with their child-rearing and homemaking roles.

Continuity of employment: the career

Some of the women who had been working most of their lives had what could be identified as a career: a succession of related positions in one or more organisations which exhibit progression in responsibility and/or remuneration. The term is used fairly loosely here since lone parents have a young age profile and are less likely than other women without partners to have progressed rapidly up an organisational hierarchy. However, there were some who were in posts which permitted them to foresee financial advancement. Often, what distinguishes a parent's career attachment is some element of initial financial sacrifice – through the need to pursue training or further education or simply spend time on a poorly remunerated rung of the career ladder – for longer-term financial benefit.

A career can provide a focus for a work orientation since it offers more of the long-term rewards (updated and transferable skills, a work-related social circle, income security in old age) than would a string of unrelated jobs. It also provides a long-term developmental focus, akin to a partnership or child-rearing role, which can provide a structure for life.

But these other roles can intervene to postpone or halt career progression, either through denying the opportunity to work, or preventing work in the locations or during the hours that a career post demands. Ruth had had to give up work when she married. She described how she rationalised the loss of a career path by concentrating on her child-rearing role.

> *First of all I resented it having to give up a job that I liked. It wasn't a brilliant career but I could probably have got promotion there ... Now I sort of feel, well it will probably do the kids good to have me here for a couple of years.*

Shirley, 42, was the mother of 7 and 19 year-old daughters, the older of whom suffered from asthma. With hindsight, Shirley regretted giving up her career when she married. Her feelings may embrace some post facto rationalisation now she was divorced, together with a more general disaffection towards her ex-husband.

> *Biggest mistake of my life! ... Because I had a brilliant job in local government. I could see promotion and even though I had no quali-fications I was recognised as having a lot of ability, the same ability as people who came out with degrees, and then [ex-husband] came on the scene and basically just told me a pack of lies, 'cos I was on a bit more salary and he could see that I had the most prospects ... So I gave up my brilliant career.*

Career goals were not restricted to those who had worked full-time since they left education. Women in low-paid part-time work – like Sandra, 23, a never-partnered mother of a five year-old who claimed Family Credit – spoke of other features of employment that persisted in their ambitions.

> *I don't want to spend all my life cleaning in the hospitals, but it does me for now. As I said, it gets me by. But once [my son] is less dependent on me I would like to go and get up and get dressed to go to work and have a job that you look forward to doing every day, things like that, rather than just going because you need the money.*

Progression on a career ladder also provided Judith, a 39 year-old never-partnered mother of a four year-old girl, with her rationale for pursuing her unrewarding current job. It was a step on the way to better things.

> *What I've been doing over the last two years, although it has been a means to an end, it's not something I'd chosen to do. It's certainly not something I'd want to carry on doing, it is for two hours a day.*

It's physically demanding and I'd like to see it as the beginning to getting on to doing more.

Sian, 41, a high-earning divorcee, talked about taking on part-time work after the split as the most she could handle. She saw this as the only way to re-enter her career once her partnership role had ended, despite the constraints of geography and child rearing.

Because looking after two small children on your own is just very time-consuming. I had quite a long [commute]. I mean there wasn't a job locally ... I look back and think 'God, how the hell did I ever do that?' but it was like a sort of foot back on the path.

and later

I wasn't prepared to let somebody else reduce me to having nothing, I saw it as a way of getting back dignity and progression.

However, career attachment and work orientation are not synonymous. Other parents, with fewer skills, were highly motivated to work and focused much more on the immediate rewards.

I've not got any training for anything. I wouldn't go to college to train for a career or anything like that. I'd want to just get out and get a job and earn. [Mary]

It's just unfortunate that I have to go on Income Support. But it's not a long-term thing as far as I'm concerned. [Rachel]

The unemployment's just so high, that if there is a job that's so good, you haven't got a very good chance: they'll always give it to somebody who's better qualified. I'm not really qualified for anything. I didn't do bad at school: I've got exams, but I've never had experience in a better job, a proper job. There's always going to be somebody out there who'll have it. I've done lots of things but I'm not really skilled. [Alison]

A very common theme among women less familiar with the labour market was low self-confidence. Moving into employment would not only demand acquisition of work-related skills, it would require a set of social skills many out-of-work women felt that they did not possess. Whereas being the parent of a young child was a more or less private role, employment would require a public performance for which those distant from the labour market were unfamiliar with the script.

Jane had very low self-esteem after her absence from the labour market. In her estimation, the world of work required her to adopt a very different set of behaviours to those she was familiar with as a mother. Implicitly, she was concerned that she would fail to live up to the expectations of other workers. Explicitly, she talked about 'carrying off' the role of a worker: she did not feel confident enough to do so.

> *I don't really want to do shop work, but when I look at myself I think well that's probably all I'm good for. If I had a better job, well if I had an interview for a better job, I wouldn't have any clothes to wear. I wouldn't be able to carry it off. I can't sort of turn up in leggings with holes in.*

Thus a major barrier to work entry was lack of confidence. Lone parents stayed with the routine they knew and felt confident performing. These were women who had established their lives around homemaking and child-rearing roles and who saw the role of a worker as alien and intimidating. The process of getting a job was viewed as similarly threatening.

> *I feel really nervous at times, but maybe because I've been sitting in for all these years. The very idea of going for an interview would send shockwaves through me.* [Emma]

> *I've got to the stage now where you need to build up confidence in yourself to work. But I suppose I worked full-time for ten years before I had the kids ... Now I've stopped for a couple of years I'd find it harder to go back into that situation, because it's just lack of confidence ... Then I feel guilty for the children, I mean there's this awful guilt, you ask a lot of working mothers and they'll say 'I feel guilty'. You shouldn't, possibly, but I still do...* [Ruth]

Sharon, 38, a mother of three, separated from a cohabitation, had been a high-earning software trainer. Her absence from the labour market meant she would be less able to take up employment.

I would have gone for a very high-paid job, which I could have done at the time, because I was qualified for it and experienced. Of course I've got the ten year break in between. I've lost the ability to say 'Yes, I'm up to date'.

Training had an important role to play. It not only provided work-related skills, but it represented a less threatening public arena into which less confident parents could venture and test social skills. Sally moved in with her parents temporarily following her separation. Through financial necessity, she contemplated work as a life role for the very first time.

We all just sat down and said 'Well, what am I going to do?'

On her parents' advice, she decided to do a 14 week secretarial course.

I hadn't got the confidence, I hadn't worked for seven years, and these were all new skills. I was going into a totally new environment. I'd never been in an office before, I didn't know what they were like.

May was less lucky in her attempts to improve her skills.

I was going to book myself and get some qualifications. Because I thought when you're on Income Support it was free. So I went up to the college to register, and I filled out the thing that said I was on Income Support, and you had to sign at the bottom 'your only form of income'. And I said, 'Well, it's not'. I said, 'I work six hours a week' ... That disqualifies you completely, you have to pay the full cost.

Thus lone parents differed considerably in their orientation to the labour market. Some, who had established work histories or had followed career paths were unable to contemplate life without work. Others, who had prioritised their child-rearing, homemaking or partnership roles found themselves in a less confident position when their partnership broke down or when the financial or emotional demands of being an out-of-work lone parent became overwhelming. The return to work (if indeed there had been any break for the former group) was more difficult for those with less well established work histories. Once the traditional family model broke down 'traditional' mothers were at a disadvantage.

This is not to argue that lone parents familiar with work avoided difficulties in trying to combine employment with sole parenthood. A work orientation simply removed the first hurdle from their journey back to work. As Joanna related, having worked before and undergone training could raise one's expectations of what work could offer. The sorts of jobs more often open to lone parents might not coincide with those expectations.

Joanna felt that the effect of returning to work, if it was an unwanted job, could impinge on her role as mother.

> *I know it sounds silly but I don't, I want to do a job that I know that I'm going to like doing. Say I was offered a really good job cashiering at Sainsbury's again and the money was good. Deep down I know it's not for me 'cos it's not what I want to do and I wouldn't be happy there. So I think I would come home, I wouldn't be in a good mood and it would spoil everything indoors.*

Thus, one of the first barriers to work entry for many lone parents was their unfamiliarity and lack of confidence with the public arena of paid work. Those who had established strong work histories before entering lone parenthood did not face such a psychological barrier, and often had the social and work-related skills that eased the return.

SOCIAL ENVIRONMENT

Child-rearing and homemaking can be viewed as private activities in contrast to the public arena of paid employment. But while a number of out-of-work lone parents did speak of loneliness and isolation, many more occupied social worlds inhabited by other lone parents. Meeting others in similar circumstances could provide a semi-public forum to discuss the dilemmas of lone parenthood. The immediate social environment could in this way act to encourage or discourage particular types of behaviour.

If the parents in a lone mother's social network are mostly combining parenting with employment, then a number of possible positive influences on the lone mother's orientation to work are possible. The social network can provide advice and information about the process of returning to work, and can positively re-inforce the lone mother's attempts to do so. There may also be a social pressure on the lone mother to conform. Conversely, if working mothers are seen to be struggling to maintain the two roles, the influences could be negative.

The influence of friends was important for Sonia, 36, a divorced mother of four (ranging in age from a 6 year-old son to a 20 year-old daughter who suffers from spina bifida) who entered work as a care worker.

> *I've got quite a few friends that have made that move, they seemed to be managing, but that's the way I did it. So I got most of the information from friends and I just decided to go in, go for it because I really wanted to work.*

Just as likely, however, was for the social environment to discourage employment if friends and acquaintances were out of work. Jill, 29, had been married, but had brought up her five year-old son and two year-old daughter while living alone. Her work experience comprised one year in a fruit shop when she left school.

> *I don't know anybody that's working.*

Carrie, 29, was a divorcee who suffered from psoriasis and arthritis – her nine year-old daughter was asthmatic. She worked 17 hours each week as a restaurant waitress.

> *All my friends are on Income Support. All of them. Or, if they're not, they've got husbands. One or the other.*

The role model offered up in large segments of society, from other lone mothers on benefit and wives of male breadwinners, is one of women out of work, dependent on others for income. The social environment will mitigate against lone mothers seeking to take up work.

Lone mothers may have been discouraged from persisting with work by sources even closer to home. Women have described situations where their parents and partners were often not supportive of their working in marriage. This early influence on their ability to work will have informed the legitimacy they attached to work and discouraged further participation.

Media stereotyping could also create an environment in which particular behaviours were frowned upon. In Alison's case, both going out to work and staying at home came under attack.

For making things a bit better for yourself and for your child, and being able to give your child what you want ... It's hard, some-times, when people ... They always look at you, and think, 'Well, leaving that babby at home with mum', and things like that. And it's not like that. You've got to play two roles. And it's juggling both roles. It annoys me because you can't win. If you stay at home all day, and live off the state, you get criticised. If you go out, and try and make things better for yourself, you get criticised the same. You can't win, really. It's just hard, 'cos you've got to play two roles.

The influence of friends, family and partners on an individual's orientation to work is perhaps the most pervasive. If the lone mother is disadvantaged by other factors too – low self confidence, poor skills – then the lack of a positive reinforcement from her social environment may be the last straw. Equally though, support from trusted sources could encourage experimentation and participation.

Again though, it is the equilibrium between child-rearing, homemaking and working roles that is being challenged. Lone mothers cannot give up their responsibilities for the first two roles. It is the preconceptions they hold and the perceptions they form of the world of work which will influence how open they are to taking on the third role.

JOB SEARCH

Before childcare is considered explicitly, and before the next chapter examines how the financial returns from working are perceived, this chapter turns finally to another hurdle in the approach to work entry. How lone mothers actually go out and look for a paid job is rarely addressed in the literature which is concerned largely with work incentives and motivation. But the process informs both.

Through searching for work, lone mothers learn of the vacancies available and will attempt to match their requirements with what is on offer. Their success rate in doing so would be expected to inform their perceptions of what work has to offer them and how well they will fit in. Motivation to work may be strongly influenced by the success or otherwise of the job search process. It is also through this route that parents learn of the financial returns on offer and are able to estimate the net economic benefits of work entry.

Job search is a time-consuming task and not one that lone parents are required to engage in as a condition of claiming Income Support. The extent of job search among the out-of-work can thus also be taken as a gauge of work orientation. The more persistent and extensive the search, the more committed the lone parent is to finding a job. Nonetheless, other factors may intervene. As parents of young children they may have very little time to devote to the job hunt and make more use of informal information networks such as friends and family. This approach also permitted those with less self-confidence an opportunity of pursuing employment within the private domain and obtaining work in potentially less threatening environments. Thus the success of the job search process specifically, and of the lone parent's return to work more generally, may be heavily dependent on the strength of the connections between the social network and the world of employment, and the quality of chosen information sources.

A typical approach to job search was adopted by Jane. She made looking for a job part of her daily routine, but nonetheless did not go out of her way to seek vacancies. She was somewhat disillusioned with employment because of the lack of vacancies.

> *If I pass the Jobcentre I do have a look in and if I'm passing the council place where they usually have a notice board, and again in stores they have a vacancy board, which very rarely has got anything on it anyway.*

Informal networks occasionally came forward with job offers. The boyfriend of Claire's sister offered her work as a cleaner at a bus station.

> *He said 'do you want it?', and at first I was a bit wary, 'cos I swore I wasn't doing cleaning again, because I always think 'I'm better than that', for some reason. Not in a nasty way. There's nothing*

wrong with it, but I had the interview and he says 'no problems' and I said 'all right I'll go for it'.

Among out-of-work lone parents, the more casual and opportunistic approach to looking for a job predominated. Unlike women with a strong work motivation who compared vacancies with each other, those less motivated compared each opportunity with their present position out of work. Their perceptions of work were informed by what their process of job search came up with. The weaker the job search, the less well work entry fared against maintenance of the status quo. Thus a vicious circle could act in which parents' perceptions of work were unlikely to be positively reinforced.

Everybody has the attitude 'You don't like the job, there's hundreds out there that'll do it!'. [Maureen]

I've been in the Jobcentre a couple of times, but everything's like what I'm doing, more or less. The hours that I can work is exactly what I'm doing. There's nothing. I've no qualifications: I left school at fifteen. There's nothing out there full-time for somebody that hasn't got any qualifications. For the last ten years I've been fetching two kids up, so I haven't got any experience at all. [Elizabeth]

In rural economies, where most low-skilled work was concentrated on seasonal or varying workloads, the concept of job search might be less salient. Meg lived in a fishing village where fish packing jobs varied with the size of the catch. She felt that decisions about whether or not she had work were made largely by the employer.

If the work's there, you've got work, but if it's slow you're on Income Support again ... it's not very practical being put on Income Support.

SUMMARY

This chapter has concentrated on lone parents' aspirations and perceived roles in life. Lone parenthood is a temporary state,

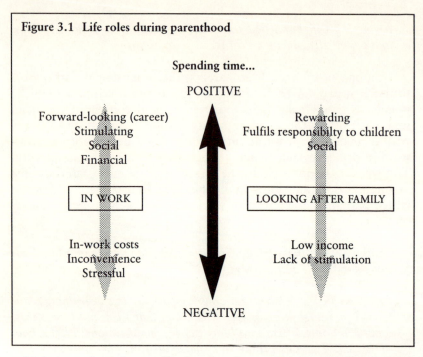

Figure 3.1 Life roles during parenthood

Spending time...

POSITIVE

Forward-looking (career)   Rewarding
Stimulating   Fulfils responsibilty to children
Social   Social
Financial

IN WORK   LOOKING AFTER FAMILY

In-work costs   Low income
Inconvenience   Lack of stimulation
Stressful

NEGATIVE

which is outlasted, usually, by the duration of parenthood, relationships and working life. It is thus parents' aspirations towards
these aspects of their lives which inform their behaviour during
lone parenthood. These goals involved spending time in homemaking, child-rearing, partnership and employment roles, each
subject to different influences. Many worked towards their model
of how to be successful in each role: to be a good parent, homemaker, wife or employee. Very few had a model of how to be a
good lone parent. The transitory state of lone parenthood induced
conflicts between families' needs and aspirations for which different solutions were sought.

This report concerns how much of a barrier is represented by
the costs and availability of childcare in lone parents' decisions.
But the costs and availability of childcare have yet to be men-
tioned. This first set of analyses have concentrated on lone parents' aspirations. The rewards and disadvantages of different life
roles as seen by lone parents are summarised in Figure 3.1. Parents
must balance the positive and negative aspects of life in or out of
work. While many parents will recognise that if they had pursued
different behaviours – stayed on in education, postponed child-

rearing or married later – they would have achieved different economic rewards, this chapter has shown that these rewards do not necessarily coincide with parents' immediate goals. If one's life role is defined by one's children, then looking after them at home may be the only way seen to fulfil it. If a life role includes career aspirations then these can be satisfied only in work. Of course some parents will be constrained from pursuing their favoured role. Some may feel that they will renege on their family commitments if they do not work to supplement their family's income. Others may want to work but be unable to find a job.

Fulfilling these aspirations may involve the use of childcare, as an end in itself – because alternative carers are seen as beneficial to the child, or as a means to an end – to enable the lone parent to take up work. As childcare allows these goals, it has been necessary to assess the strength of these goals before the role played by the availability and affordability of one of their facilitators can be identified. For those lone parents who have based their decision to stay at home on the role model set by their own family or friends, on their perceptions of what constitutes good mothering or on the poor quality of the vacancies they have identified, a barrier to work entry has been erected long before considerations of the cost of childcare come into play.

Thus, in the terms of the equation of financial and non-financial gains and losses described in Chapter 1, certain behaviours will involve greater losses for some lone parents than for others. A family-orientated parent will place a high value on time the family is together. Because her motivation to work is low the incentive needs to be higher for entry into work to find favour. A career-orientated mother will be more likely to regard a break in employment as a loss.

But the analysis in this chapter has added another dimension to the equation. Some parents are simply placed further away from considering the equation than others. The recently separated lone mother cannot contemplate time apart from her children, let alone what it is worth in a motivation-incentive equation. Likewise, a mother who until recently defined her life roles in terms of child-rearing and homemaking may be ill-equipped to consider how much she would value an additional income in return for time apart from her children. These lone mothers are more distant from the equation. They may come to consider the social and financial benefits of going out to work in due course but are unable to do so at present.

Nonetheless, lone parents with a strong work motivation have been identified, as have those who are considering returning to work for reasons of financial necessity or because they see it as a way of expanding social horizons. For these the costs and availability of childcare may well play an important part in their decisions about when they can work, for how long and at what rates of pay. The part played by childcare costs in the incentives offered by entry into work are considered in the next chapter.

Chapter 4

In-work Costs and Work Incentives

Paid employment should be financially rewarding. With the exception of mortgage holders, a minority among lone parents, the benefit system is structured to preserve a financial incentive to work. Lone parents should be better off financially if they work at least 16 hours each week than if they work fewer hours, or none at all. The structure should ensure an additional return for every additional hour of work supplied above 16. However, for many different reasons, lone parents may not perceive this incentive, or have strong grounds for believing that it does not hold in their case.

In-work costs commonly discourage optimism that work will yield a profit. Parents feel that, in order to work, they must incur additional expenditure which undermines the financial reward from work. Childcare costs are the most frequently cited among these in-work costs, but there are others such as clothing, travel and the reinstatement of demands for debt repayments frozen while out of work.

In seeking work, the lone parent is preparing to sell her labour for a wage. If she is seeking a financial reward from doing so, then there will be some minimum level of exchange below which she feels it is not worth donating her time and effort. Such parents may simply feel it is not worth working if the rate of pay for each hour worked – or the effective net rate of pay after in-work benefits have been added and income tax and national insurance taken away – is so low that the return on each hour worked fails to meet the value she places on her time.

These are the incentive debates which labour economists model (for example, Duncan, 1990; Duncan, Giles and Webb, 1995), and the effect of which sociologists, psychologists and economists attempt to interpret (see Bryson and McKay (eds) 1994; White (ed) 1994). It is also the principal potential barrier to labour market participation which successive policy initiatives have attempted to redress. The interrelationship of in-work and out-of-work benefits, the disregards on certain portions of income, and bonus payments have been designed to enable lone parents and others who wish to do so, to be able to secure an income in work which exceeds the benefit income they could expect out of work.

One of these disregards, as introduced in 1994, ignores the first £40 of income spent on professional childcare for a child or children aged under 11 years in income assessable for in-work benefits. Lone parents working 16 hours or more each week are the principal group eligible for this disregard. From April 1996, the disregard value is increased to £60.

In order to illustrate the effect of the disregard on work incentives, it is worth describing in some detail the financial world lone parents inhabit: how benefits interact at different numbers of hours supplied, and how childcare costs impinge on the return from work with and without the disregard.

LONE PARENTS' BUDGET CONSTRAINTS

In-work means-tested benefits are designed with tapers which mean that increases in earnings are partially offset by a reduction in benefit entitlement. Earning more should result in higher net income, while at the same time the level of benefit is reduced. This should provide the incentive for potential recipients to work more hours. An example is given in Figure 4.1 which shows the different sources of income and benefit entitlement a lone parent with one young child can draw upon at any given number of hours worked each week. When in work, this 'model' lone parent receives the median rate of pay per hour lone parents earn in work – £3.66 per hour.[1] She is also liable for median rent and maximum council tax of £37.50 and £6.28 per week, respectively, and receives £10 each week in maintenance. Out of work she is entitled to maximum Income Support (less One Parent Benefit (OPB) and any maintenance received). Upon starting work, she can keep each pound of income earned from work up to the level of the earnings disregard for Income Support (£15). Thus, assuming no additional costs due to being in work (in this example childcare is

Figure 4.1 Lone parent income by hours worked: benefit rates as at November 1994

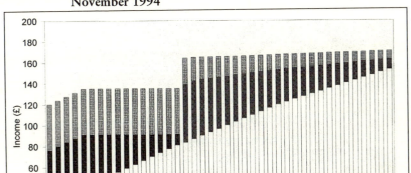

assumed to be provided free), there is a financial incentive to work more hours, up to five, each week. After that, each extra pound earned is deducted pound for pound from Income Support. She sees the same net income working for 15 hours each week as she does working for five.

By working 16 or more hours each week, the lone parent becomes eligible for Family Credit, which has a disregard on maintenance of up to £15 each week. At 1994 rates, she is entitled to maximum Family Credit of £55.50 for as long as she earns £71.70 or less each week. The award of Family Credit produces a considerable increase in income of nearly £30 each week. Family Credit is included in the assessable income against which Housing Benefit (HB) and Council Tax Benefit (CTB) entitlement is calculated. From this point on, Housing Benefit is reduced by 65 per cent, and Council Tax Benefit by 20 per cent, for every extra pound of assessable income.

Without Family Credit, the family would be exposed to what is commonly termed the 'unemployment trap': final incomes smaller in work than those available on Income Support out of work. The trap can still exist if in-work costs (travel, clothing, childcare) are high, and can be substantial for people who are buying their own homes. There is no help with mortgage interest payments available to those who work 16 hours or more.

Once the lone parent is earning above her Family Credit threshold of £71.70 (in this example, reached by working 18 hours each week or more), the 70 per cent taper on Family Credit against assessable earned income comes into effect. Taken together with National Insurance contributions, until her entitlement to Council Tax Benefit expires, the parent sees a net income gain of about 15p for every extra hour worked above 15. This represents a marginal withdrawal or 'tax' rate on earnings of 96 per cent. This small financial gain from working more hours produces the 'poverty trap'. There is a financial incentive to work more hours, but a very small one.

It can also be argued that a low financial return from working cannot recompense losses sustained in non-financial ways. The lone parent may value her time at an hourly rate higher than the net return from work less the Income Support she would have received out of work. She may certainly value it more highly than the net hourly return of 15p illustrated above. But she is unlikely to look at work in this way. A more realistic comparison is the net gain from working 16, 24 or 35 hours compared to none or 5 (Table 4.1).

Table 4.1 Financial incentive to work different numbers of hours for 'model' lone parent (see text)

	Number of hours worked			
	5	16	24	35
Return (in £ per week) from each *additional hour worked compared to:*				
Out of work	3.00	2.77	1.93	1.41
Working five hours		2.67	1.64	1.15
Working 16 hours			0.23	0.27
Working 24 hours				0.29

Table 4.1 shows that how the 'model' lone parent with the potential to earn £3.66 an hour views the incentive for working more hours depends very much on her starting point. Movement into work of 5, 16 or 24 hours each week is quite attractive (if mea-

sured in terms of return per additional hour worked) if she is out of work. She will receive the majority of every additional pound she earns. Movement into work of 16 hours each week is also attractive when viewed from working five hours each week. However, the effect of benefit tapers is to make the return on each additional hour look very poor if the lone parent is already working 16 hours or more.

A 'rational' lone parent whose choice of work was determined solely by incentives might thus be expected to select work of 16 hours each week and have little cause to work more hours. Indeed, this is the modal number of hours worked by lone parents who claim Family Credit and the average is only 25 hours. Nonetheless, a number of factors may intervene to disrupt this rational approach. The first is that not all lone parents follow the 'model' lone parent's example and claim all the benefits to which they are entitled. Likewise, they may not be entitled to the same range of benefits. A lone parent who is not eligible for Housing Benefit or Council Tax Benefit (perhaps because she owns her home outright) will see more of every pound she earns when working more than 16 hours, because these benefit tapers will not apply (a steeper slope applies in Figure 4.1 when the Housing Benefit and Council Tax Benefit amounts are ignored). This increased incentive comes at the price of a lower total income before housing costs. Mortgage buyers receive no help with housing costs if they work 16 hours or more each week. To achieve the same final incomes after housing costs as renters, mortgage payers require higher earnings.

The second factor is that lone parents are not fully aware of the benefit tapers that apply to the work they do. In the National Survey, only 15 per cent of lone parent Family Credit claimants knew that the benefit was withdrawn at the rate of 70p for every extra pound earned. Knowledge of the withdrawal rate was even lower among non-recipients. Lone parents see an income from work, and if their circumstances change, or they work more hours, their next claim produces another income. They are quite likely to compare the two, but they will not be fully aware of their financial position in a situation they have yet to experience. Knowledge of incentives will be based largely on their own past experience, their observations of what others have received, and the advice of Benefits Agency staff and welfare rights workers. However well they recall such details, they will not be basing their decision on

whether or not to enter work in an environment of perfect knowledge. Some will take a job and simply hope for the best.

The third factor is the extent to which lone parents actually
supply labour in response to a nominal net gain per hour worked.
Where the motive for taking up work is the pursuit of the social
rewards of employment, or to preserve long-term contact with the
labour market for career reasons, the return per hour may be a
secondary consideration. Even lone mothers motivated by financial necessity may seek an absolute rather than a relative gain from
employment. If the model lone mother is out of work and wants
to increase her income by £50, she must move into work of 38
hours or more each week. Arguments that 90 per cent of this
increase could be earned from just 18 hours work may hold little
weight if £50 is what she really needs.

Finally, incentives rarely work in the simple way modelled here.
Rates of pay are likely to differ with the hours of work supplied.
Full-time work may offer fringe benefits that part-time work does
not. Lone parents may find that their ex-partner reduces his maintenance contributions to take account of her higher income. Many
factors will intervene to complicate the relationship between modelled incentives and final income.

Within this last set of factors must be included in-work costs.
These may vary in a uniform way with number of hours worked,
like childcare charges by the hour. Alternatively the relationship
between in work costs and hours supplied may be non-uniform,
such as the requirement for capital outlay on clothes or equip-
ment, or travel costs, which may vary with the number of working
days or shifts and vary with the timing of journeys.

The situation described so far ignores any additional costs arising from being in work. Expenditure on childcare or travel may
effectively remove the financial incentive to work longer hours.
Before October 1994, any payments lone parents made for childcare represented an irrecoverable loss from income. Typically,
childcare costs rise incrementally with each hour worked: a parent
working 20 hours a week pays out twice as much for care as one
working 10 hours. If the lone parent modelled in Figure 4.1 has to
pay £0.88 for childcare each hour she is in work, the effect on net
income is quite dramatic.[2] Figure 4.2 shows that paying for childcare by the hour accentuates both the 'poverty' and 'unemployment' traps. The gain for each additional hour worked is reduced,
and is negative across much of the hours distribution (Table 4.2).

Table 4.2   **Financial incentive to work different numbers of hours for 'model' lone parent with hourly childcare cost of £0.88, without childcare disregard**

	Number of hours worked			
	5	16	24	35
Return (in £ per week) from each additional hour worked compared to:				
Out of work	2.12	1.89	1.05	0.53
Working five hours		1.79	0.76	0.27
Working 16 hours			-0.65	-1.30
Working 24 hours				-0.59

In Figure 4.2, the amount of earned income is used to assess benefit entitlements just as before. The lone parent receives exactly the same entitlements to benefit in Figure 4.2 as Figure 4.1. Once childcare costs have been deducted from earnings, however, net increases in earnings per hour worked are too low to compensate for the withdrawal of benefits, national insurance and income tax.

Figure 4.2   **Lone parent income by hours worked after childcare costs**

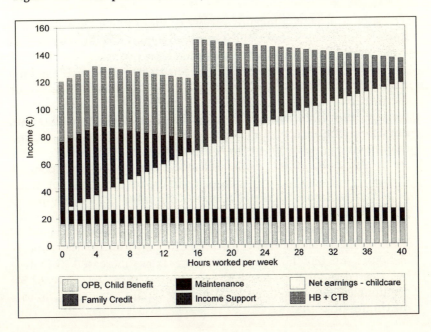

**Figure 4.3   Lone parent income with child care allowance: other benefit
rates as at November 1994**

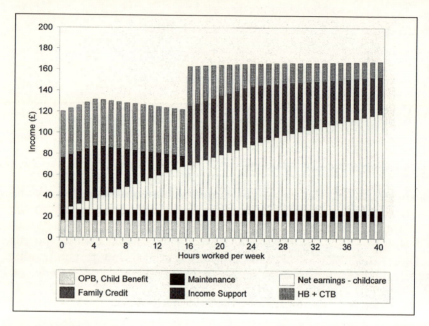

There is no financial incentive to work more hours than the minimum which brings about entitlement to Family Credit. There is, in
effect, a disincentive to work any longer each week.

The childcare disregard acts to restore the incentive for lone
parents of children aged under 11 years, working 16 hours or
more each week and who pay for childcare, provided care is
sought from professional sources (registered childminders and
nurseries). Childcare costs (up to £40 each week)[3] are deducted
from income assessable for means-tested benefits of those in work
16 hours or more each week. The effect this has on net income is
shown in Figure 4.3. The income profile up to 16 hours each week
is unchanged from Figure 4.2, as the disregard does not apply to
part-time work. In work 16 hours or more, the childcare disregard
reduces the amount of income assessable for means-tested benefits.
Thus, earned income less childcare costs per hour are the same as
in Figure 4.2 but the benefit entitlements are increased. It is as if
her earned income as assessed for Family Credit was only £2.78
per hour (£3.66 earned per hour less £0.88 childcare costs, up to a
maximum of £40).

In Figure 4.3, our 'model' lone parent working 16 hours each week thus becomes entitled to maximum Family Credit. She remains entitled to maximum Family Credit working up to 23 hours per week. Once her net earnings less childcare exceed £71.70, the Family Credit taper comes into effect and she has 70p taken off this maximum for every pound increase in net earnings less childcare. An incentive to work more hours, in the form of increased net income, is high at 16 hours, when entitled to maximum benefits, but is reduced at 24 hours work, as the taper on Family Credit comes into effect.

The above example shows that, because the qualifying threshold for Family Credit is set on higher earnings, the principal source of increased in-work benefit following the introduction of a childcare disregard will be Family Credit. Nevertheless, for many with low earnings and high rents, it is not the only source. In order to benefit fully from the disregard, lone parents must claim each of up to three means-tested benefits to which they become or remain entitled: Family Credit, Housing Benefit and Council Tax Benefit. Depending on their circumstances, the childcare disregard could produce increases in their entitlements in any one, two or in all three. It is thus possible for a lone parent paying for childcare to be entitled to the same Family Credit after the introduction of the disregard as before, but more Housing Benefit. This is the case in our example (Figures 4.2 and 4.3). Working 16 or 17 hours each week, she receives maximum Family Credit under both new and old rules, because her assessable earned income, regardless of whether she pays for childcare, is below the threshold of £71.70. The increase in income following the rule change results from increased Housing Benefit entitlement.

There may be considerable problems posed for take-up if a lone parent who enters work and pays for childcare fails to realise that she will be compensated for childcare costs by deductions from her rent. Under the new rules, if she enters work from Income Support it will appear that she simply *continues* to receive most of her rent rebate, whereas in work under the old rules she had to meet more of her housing costs from the rest of her income. There may be problems convincing lone parents who contemplate entering work of 16 hours each week that the additional benefit they will derive from paying £14.08 each week for childcare on entering work is that due to having to pay £9.15 less in rent each week and £2.81 less in Council Tax than they would otherwise. The childcare disregard thus, in theory, restores an incentive for lone parents paying for professional childcare to work longer hours and increase the proportion of their income which is earned. The role played by the disregard, in reality, will depend upon the intentions of lone parents to work, or work longer hours, their likely earnings, their intended source and costs of childcare and the extent to which they become aware of, and claim, means-tested benefits while in work.

THE NEED FOR MORE INCOME

Incentive arguments are based on neo-classical consumer theory (Bryson and McKay, 1994). People will seek to maximise the utility of work through the selection of jobs and hours which produce a maximum yield for minimum effort. The budget constraints above illustrate that a typical lone parent has access to a non-labour income after housing costs of around £80. The incentives question is thus how much more income does a lone parent require to give up some of her non-labour time to paid work.

Economists make reference to an income effect which suggests that as a person's income increases, their desire to work more hours declines, because they wish for time in which to spend their income. The lower a person's non-work income, the more earnings they should need before the income effect applies. As a lone parent's non-work income is comprised largely of Income Support, there should be some incentive to increase income through entry into work. The implication is that those who have most to gain from additional income will have the greatest incentive to enter work.

Monetary gain should act as a strong incentive for parents to enter work. They will be quite some way up the income scale before the income effect applies. They may not be in work because they feel they have to sacrifice a great deal to take up paid work. But there is little doubt from these accounts that lone parents have a lot to gain from additional income.

This was not a study of the hardship lone parents experience out of work, nor of the benefits they perceived could flow from additional income. Nonetheless, the majority of interviews included some discussion of the financial problems lone parents faced on a day-to-day basis: meeting regular and unexpected expenditures, making each giro last the week, their reliance on second hand clothes or hand-me-downs and problems with debt. For lone parents out of work for some time, the persistence of these problems was evidenced in a combination of monotonous frugality and persistent anxiety.

New Year's worse, because we've started a new year, and you're thinking I just couldn't have another year like last year. Not that anything particularly bad happened last year, but it's just the struggling ... I think I've done awful well getting by. We've survived January. February's a nice short month, so we're laughing. The birthday's coming up in April, so the pressure starts. [Maureen]

My winter coat this year: I swapped with my sister for one of my other coats which was lighter, so I swapped her that and [my son], he gets like hand-downs from a friend. [Eileen]

There was a considerable contrast between the depth interviewees who were in work of 16 or more hours each week and those who were not working these hours when questioned in the National Survey. When asked how they were managing financially, a third of those in work felt they were managing very well or quite well, compared to just one in 12 out-of-work. Likewise, among the out of work, two-thirds declared themselves to be worried about money nearly all the time, compared to a third of workers.

Subjective accounts of life outside of work were not favourable. If paid work could supply additional income to these families, there would seem to be a considerable incentive for out-of-work parents to take up work and increase their income. However, one counterintuitive finding among depth interviewees was that those most likely to be worried about money when asked in the National Survey were those out of work who had *not* been seeking work in the past year. Those who were seeking work were much *less* likely to see themselves as badly off. There could be many explanations for such a finding:

- those seeking work may be motivated by factors other than financial necessity;
- those who choose to seek work may differ in other ways (skills, self-confidence), which make them more optimistic in their answers, from those who were not seeking;

- those who choose to seek work may have higher non-work incomes, due in part to the receipt of maintenance, which make them better off;

- those seeking work were less likely to have spent a long time out of work, and many fewer will have experienced long-term hardship out of work.

The explanations suggest a problem of levels. Although all the out-of-work respondents had low enough incomes to respond to any financial incentive offered by work, those in the greatest difficulty were least well equipped with qualifications and experience to work, and knew it. If the level of financial anxiety is not closely related to the decision to seek work, then financial incentives may be less effective in helping lone parents into work. Other problems which distance those not seeking work from the labour market need to be addressed first. By the same reasoning, however, the absence of a financial incentive, an absence arising due to the cost of childcare, for example, might not act as a barrier to employment.

This is to dissociate somewhat an understanding of the financial implication of work entry from its effect on lone parents' work intentions. The following part of this chapter will focus on lone parents' awareness of the financial gains and losses associated with taking up work of different hours. The permutations of available jobs, skills match, hours of work, their location during the day, corresponding benefit entitlements and different in-work costs, especially the costs of childcare are numerous and complex. Finding out how much lone parents know about the financial consequences of each permutation is a necessary, but not a sufficient, condition for us to understand the role that financial incentives play in the decision to work. We also need to know how much financial differentials mean to them, what it is that makes the difference between attractive and unattractive income packages in work. This will be examined in the final part of the chapter.

It has been argued elsewhere that low income families are very rarely fully aware of their own budget constraint (Marsh, 1994). They may be unsure about the net earnings any particular job will produce and are unlikely to understand fully how benefit entitlements are calculated. The incentive is thus measured less in net gain per hour worked, than a comparison of discrete situations: past experiences in work, their current financial situation, and likely future income in each job among the range of vacancies they are aware of at any one time. They may calculate this themselves, or ask others for advice. The full implications, after in-work costs have been taken into account, are unlikely to be realised until after the job has been started.

Awareness of the benefit system among lone parents is not perfect. Nearly all know about Income Support. The simple system whereby one pound of benefit is withdrawn for each pound in income earned was understood by most, as was the £15 disregard on earnings. Most are also aware of the existence of Family Credit, though only a few are clear as to how it works or of its relationship with other in-work benefits such as Housing Benefit and Council Tax Benefit. Surprisingly, many who knew of a way in which they could become entitled to Family Credit, did not actually know why they became entitled. Josie, for example, whose work experience extended to four weeks as a cleaner, saw it as a supplement for part-time work. She did not think it would cover low-paid full-time employment.

> *If I did get a full-time job they'd only take my Income Support off me. So if I got a job for say £80 a week, they'd take £66 a week off me, so I'd be working for fourteen pound ... I'd be working for next to nothing. It'd be pointless me getting a full-time job ... So I'd really be better off with something part-time and claim Family Credit.*

The pound for pound withdrawal of Income Support beyond the first £15 earned meant Joanna was unwilling to take up longer part-time hours which were less than the minimum required to claim Family Credit. She interpreted the absence of financial gain as a loss.

> *I worked as a lunchtime supervisor, and they even offered me work over there, to help out in the class. But because of my Income Support I couldn't do it 'cos I would have lost too much. It wasn't enough, it wasn't more than 16 hours so I couldn't do that either. So I just went back to the cleaning.*

Perhaps more important, those who wanted to reintroduce themselves to work by taking a part-time job, were dissuaded by the 100 per cent marginal tax rate on Income Support, after the first £15 of earned income. Maggie, 36 and a divorced mother of three, felt she was struggling on Income Support and wanted to secure more earned income. She had done office and shop work but stopped with the arrival of her first child.

> *There would be no benefit to me going out and having a little job, 'cos they would deduct it from my Income Support pound for pound that I earn.*

It has been argued that lone parents are more aware of the benefit system than any other client group, because so many are actually receiving benefits. The higher take-up rate for Family Credit among lone parents compared to couples is in part attributed to this awareness (Marsh and McKay, 1993b). Yet among lone parents, knowledge of how Family Credit was withdrawn varies in its sophistication. Most are aware that higher earnings mean less or no Family Credit in any new award, but are less certain of the effect on final take home income. A surprisingly high proportion of those who talked of taking better paid jobs, thought the loss of Family Credit would leave them worse off. Of course, unless they were particularly heavy users of Family Credit passport benefits such as free prescriptions and dental fees, a better paid job should always leave them better off.

> *If I went for a better job then I'd lose my Family Credit.* [Sonia]

> *You get a pay rise, and you're not happy about it, 'cos you know it's going to affect your benefit, and you'll probably be worse off. Not just equal. You just don't equal out. A lot of the time, it makes you worse off. So you think, 'When's it ever going to end?' You never seem to be able to better yourself'.* [Alison]

Some of this perception could be because entitlements are held constant for six months. A pay rise or move into a better job between claims would not affect the amount of Family Credit received until the next claim. Combined weekly income immediately after the new claim had been processed might well represent an improvement on net income immediately after the previous claim (six months before), but look much less favourable compared to income received just one week before.

Of course, most lone parents do not have the opportunity to experiment with the effects of increasing earnings on their own

Family Credit claim. They must look elsewhere to learn about the consequences of claiming Family Credit, in many cases to the experiences of other lone parents in their social network. Around half the out-of-work lone parents had done so, but recognised that the impact of combining earnings and Family Credit was difficult to discern outside the 'black box' of others' management of their household budgets.

Joanna felt that she would need a well-paid job if Family Credit was to work for her. She based her view in part on the experiences of her friend.

> *She's no better off at all. She must earn quite a bit of money, but she doesn't get a lot of Family Credit. Whether she doesn't manage it or what, I don't really know.*

Jean, 38, was a divorced mother who lived with her two sons. One was a disruptive 12 year-old. The other, aged 19, had recently stopped work. Jean had worked in a sock factory and a sweet factory. She had already made it clear that she would only seek work to improve her financial circumstances. She was especially concerned by the apparent loss of Housing Benefit and free school dinners when claiming Family Credit.

> *They've actually to pack it in because they couldn't afford to pay all their rent ... [On Income Support] you don't pay rent. Off the Social she gets sixty odd pound a week. She was only £5 for her electric and the rest of that was all hers. Now she's out working, I don't know how much wages she gets, but she can't afford to pay all her rent because she's to pay for somebody to get the kid after school. She's to pay the kid's hot dinners – you don't get a free dinner.*

Jean was less concerned about childcare costs herself because she already had a free source of childcare of her own.

Maggie, a mother of three, was seeking work but said she would feel very insecure off Income Support if her pay was not sufficient. Again, her financial anxieties stemmed from a friend's experiences.

> *She's also struggling. She's got two children and for a while she worked. We sat down and actually worked out her earnings compared to what she get on benefits, it didn't pay her to work.*

Other parents turned to more formal advisers such as the Benefits Agency. Even here, advice could be confused, or confusing, if there was no concrete job opportunity to evaluate. Ruth was concerned that her CSA-assessed maintenance was about to lift her off Income Support, which would make her liable for her mortgage interest payments.

> *I was going to go back to the pool and do a part-time job and checked what it would be with the DSS – about Family Credit. And they only say to you, 'Either get married again or find yourself a partner, and you have to go out full-time. Otherwise, don't bother', and that's their advice to you. I don't particularly want to get married again. It took me three years to get out of me last one.*

She agreed with their advice on full-time work, however. The benefit tapers were such that to meet her additional in-work costs, mortgage interest payments and childcare, she would have to secure a high level of earnings.

So although the lone mothers interviewed were largely aware of the availability of in-work benefits, they were less certain about their effects in their own case, and they were poorly informed to discuss their role in decisions about work in the abstract. The majority of friends offered poor examples of how Family Credit might help them, although only a handful of mothers were willing to extrapolate others' experiences directly onto their own situation.

Elizabeth was working five hours each week to take advantage of the Income Support disregard during school hours. When she found a vacancy for 16 or more hours' shift work, she sought advice from her welfare rights office.

> *It would have meant I was £10.04 a week better off, but it would've cost me that to get sitters in for the kids, so it wasn't worth it. So I don't see that it would be worth me working full-time unless I was going to be £200 a week or something like that. 'Cos I would've got £48.96 from work, and £66 Family Credit plus me Child Benefit, then after all me deductions I would have to pay Council Tax, so much towards my rent. I'd lose out on the free school meals.*

She could not claim the childcare disregard because no registered childminder was prepared to cover her shiftwork hours.

WHAT DO FINANCIAL DIFFERENTIALS MEAN?

Once in work, parents may choose to work more hours only if the wage rate itself improves. This is what economists call a 'substitution effect' (Laidler, 1981) because income is substituting for leisure. The budget constraints illustrated in Figures 4.1 to 4.3 are based on a constant wage rate. Typically, however, the more hours employees work per week, the more they receive from their employers per hour. Because lone mothers compete alongside others in the labour market they should share in this better rate of pay the more hours they work.

However, the lone mother may not benefit fully from higher wage rates. The effect of the benefit tapers and in-work costs such as childcare which apply to lone mothers may temper the increases in effective wage rates. In such situations, lone parents may not see any incentive to work more hours. Parents may not understand how entering work would affect them because they have little idea of their likely income and outgoings. There are too many variables in the equation. Janine sums up her own situation and that of many out-of-work lone parents when she recognises that her low level of skills and inexperience are unlikely to secure work which would enable her to meet her aspirations of leaving Income Support.

I'm not qualified or experienced enough to earn a decent wage, to come off the Social Security. No one's going to want to pay someone that's inexperienced. Even after a three-month trial period, and training, I've got to be doing a good job, and I've got to be really good at that job, to pick up minimum £160 a week. 'Cos, straightaway, dentist bills, prescriptions, school meals, rent, rates. All that. I probably wouldn't have to pay all of it, but even half of each, of everything, would mount up. And it's no good paying for all that, and then finding out I'm worse off ... Because I've got no experience behind me, and I can't ever see myself gaining any experience, to stay in a good job, and to get a good wage, it is off-putting. I don't want to go on the government pay-roll for the rest of my life. I want to go out. I want a house. I want things for my kids. I want a swing in the garden. Silly things like that. I know I've got to go out and get it. But at the same time, the world's got to be half-way to meet me. I can't do it all on my own.

No matter how much labour Janine was prepared to supply, she could not foresee an earned income which would compensate for the in-work costs she would face. This was her judgement. But however realistic she was in assessing her earning power, she did not allow for any supplementation of her likely wages with Family Credit, although she was aware of its existence. Of course, without any means-tested supplement, the poverty trap should appear less daunting, because she would expect to keep more of each pound she earned. But the poverty trap was not the issue. What mattered to her decision was that without taking into account such a supplement she could not conceive herself earning an amount sufficient to substitute for her income claiming Income Support plus her in-work costs.

In-work costs posed the main barrier for Rebecca too, a 36 year-old mother of two (youngest aged six years), separated from marriage and keen to work. She had worked as a dental nurse for seven years and on a cancer ward, but most recently had taken sub-post office work to fit her son's school hours. She saw no incentive to work after taking into account in-work costs. The opportunity cost of missing time with her children also entered the equation.

> *It's not attractive being on Income Support by any means but they leave you in that trap where if you're earning too much all your benefits go. So you may end up with the same amount. You may be slogging your guts out 40 hours a week and still ending up with as little as you were getting on Income Support. Who's going to try? No one's going to try. I mean only for your own self-preservation, but for the actual love of work itself. I don't think anyone's going to put themselves out that much and miss out on their families growing up for the sake of it.*

The problems were perceived in much the same way by those in work. Cynth, a 36 year-old divorcee, had just started to do bar work and claim Family Credit. She paid her 14 year-old daughter to look after her two younger children in the evenings. She was not optimistic about her final income, since her entitlement to Housing Benefit had yet to be calculated.

> *Me being on the social is costing them money, but at the same time you try to get yourself off the social and it still costs you money,*

> *but it's like a catch-22. They give you money and they take from the other, so you're never going to be any better off realistically. I mean it's like I had my rent and that paid, now I'm going to have to pay something, but I'm still going to be back to square one ... Once they work out the rent, I don't honestly think I'm going to be better off. Not at all. Even though I am working, and it's not that bad a paid job really for what I do.*

Eileen had dropped out of full-time work since we first met her. She had enjoyed the work and her reason for leaving was the availability of childcare for her one year-old infant rather than any financial disincentive. Nonetheless, she felt she had not gained financially from work, even with the childcare disregard applied to her Housing Benefit.

> *I'm on the same money now as what I was when I was working. I mean when I was working, it got me into debt more. I had a child-minder to pay and me house as well and me bus fares and dinners. So I'm no better off or worse off being on the social.*

The phrase 'Catch-22' was used by at least three respondents to describe their predicament contemplating work entry. For Maggie, a mother of three, the familiar list of in-work costs was topped again by anxieties about Housing Benefit. Lack of knowledge of how benefit entitlements were calculated meant that the final income from work was unknown. Work entry was a step in the dark which, in their eyes, offered as much potential for loss as for gain.

> *I feel as though I'm in a Catch-22 that I can't actually do anything for myself because of what I would lose. So I'm frightened of how much rent I'd have to find, council tax have to pay for, all the children's school dinners. They sound like silly things but the kids have school dinners that's £15 a week.*

It was lack of knowledge rather than false perceptions which were key. Among lone parent renters in the National Survey, those on Income Support were much less likely to be certain that Housing Benefit could be paid to those in work of 16 hours or more. Only a quarter of non-claimants did not know this. But nearly half those on Income Support had no idea whether or not it was available and 5 per cent thought it definitely was not. Surprisingly, 22 per cent of Family Credit renters similarly did not know Housing Benefit could be paid to them.

Thus for Marie who had no idea of the availability of Housing Benefit in work, the main in-work cost was rent.

> *It's got to be full-time, otherwise, it's not worth going to work, is it? It would have to be a job where it's very well-paid, because once you've got a job, you've got to pay your rent.*

It was easier for mortgage payers to *know* the extent of the financial incentive offered by paid work. Janet was working part-time and saw no incentive in changing her situation. She kept her wages below the Income Support threshold to ensure her mortgage interest payments were met through Income Support. Her boss was keen for her to work full-time, but she was convinced that such a move would not be worth her while financially as her effective hourly wage rate would drop.

> *I work more hours, I lose out financially, I mean, there's quite a lot of us, if you go on to Family Credit you get no help with the mortgage ... I could get 35 hours tomorrow. My boss wants me to work more.*

Facing what she perceived to be a negative return on additional hours worked, Janet remained on Income Support. Although she enjoyed her job she was not prepared to pay for the privilege of doing it. In some ways, however, she was lucky to have the choice. Not only was she facing a concrete job opportunity against which she could assess the incentives, she had a clear idea of what her in-work costs would be as she was already there, working part-time. The effect of working 16 or more hours on help with housing costs is also easier for home buyers to predict. The tapers and income thresholds applicable to Housing Benefit do not apply: mortgage interest payments are simply withdrawn.

It is important to note that these perceptions of a lack of an incentive to work are not representative of lone mothers' attitudes to the financial returns from work. The sample contained workers only if they had entered their jobs in the past year. Such a sample is more likely to contain those for whom the financial case for working is more marginal, since those who gain financially from work tend to stay there year on year (Ford, Marsh and Finlayson, 1996 forthcoming). Representative samples of lone parents with experience of life on Family Credit and on Income Support tend to favour the former.

Almost by definition, most lone mothers in work felt better off there in some way. If they did not, they were unlikely to stay there. Carrie was on the borderline, she saw little financial return and had run up debts but felt work contributed to her self-esteem. She would have worked more hours if her mother had been available as a source of childcare.

> *Most days, I'm thinking it's all right, it's better than living on the Social. But then, the stressful days, I think, this just isn't worth it.*

Meg, who had been in work on maximum Family Credit until she was laid off, said she was much better off in work.

> *I used to borrow off [my mum] quite a lot but that was when I was on Income Support. When I was on Family Credit, everybody seemed to be borrowing off me.*

Julie, 37, who had worked as a secretary in Ethiopia before she came to Britain, had separated from her marriage. She now did very occasional restaurant work. She left rent rebate out of the picture when she was offered full-time work. As her council rent was £72 each week, absence of such knowledge made a big difference to her perception of incentives.

> *They said 'If you want a full-time job, you've got one because I'm happy with you'. I asked him how much he would give me every week and the hours that I'd be doing. I said to him 'Wait, let me find out'. A friend of mine said if you work over 16 hours you can get Family Credit, depending on how much you earn. So I worked it all out and I was only better off about £40.*

Parents have different expectations. In rejecting a £40 bonus for being in work, Julie has rejected an amount higher than the typical differential between in-work and out-of-work income for lone parents who claim all to which they are entitled. Yet, an increase in final income of little more made such a big difference to Susan that she felt the DSS had made a mistake in her favour. The £15 disregard on maintenance in Family Credit assessable income meant she received a high award of Family Credit: £46 more than her Income Support.

> *It's a huge difference to me, like when I was on Income Support they were only giving me something like, they reduced it, it went back to about £23 a week or something ridiculous. And then when I went onto Family Credit they gave me £69 and I was earning money and I couldn't understand it.*

The difference in these mothers' perceptions was not accounted for by family size: both Susan and Julie had large families – four children each. But childcare could have made a difference. Julie was planning to pay her cousins £25 each week to care for her children while Susan was able to let her older children care for her younger ones for free.

Elaine noticed a drop in her final income after she was laid off and her Family Credit claim came to an end. As she was also one of the few lone mothers we interviewed who received maintenance, the maintenance disregard may have made the difference.

> *I found it a lot harder since I came on to Income Support which only changed two weeks ago ... I was on Family Credit because it lasts for the full six months, so even though I'm not actually paying rent now I find it is harder. I've noticed. Not that much of a difference but I've noticed a difference.*

For some mothers, like Julie, the size of the incentive seemed to be all important, whereas for others, like Elaine, cash differences seemed to matter less. Sonia, too, as a mortgage payer should have seen high in-work costs as she had to meet her mortgage interest payments. She had made the decision to work after much deliberation then felt worse off, which she attributed to school bus fares and council tax rather than having to pay mortgage interest.

> *It did put me off for a long time: going into work full-time, the thought of coming off Income Support, going onto Family Credit and 'would I really be able to manage on that?' ... I was better off on Income Support ... Money. Everything, I got the kids free dinners. I was able to take them to school because I wasn't working. Now I have to give them bus fares because I'm working. I have to*

pay council tax now, and it's just everything really ... I don't think I can go back onto Income Support because I'd have given up my job. And you're not allowed Income Support are you?

Sonia's misunderstanding of lone parents' unconditional entitlement to Income Support when out of work meant she felt trapped in an unrewarding job. This could affect her willingness to experiment with different jobs in future.

Incentives are measured by comparing net *amounts* of money received for different hours supplied. Accordingly, most parents who felt better or worse off attributed this to differences in their final income. However, some mothers, like Sandra, were less concerned with the actual amounts than with the way Family Credit contributed to their management of the family budget.

> *I've never actually sat down and worked it out, but I like the way it works out. I get my Family Credit on a Tuesday and I pay everything. That gets me round to the Friday and then I get my wages, so I don't think I could go back to just having the book and nothing at the weekend. I would just, I would never get by then I don't think, I'd be up to here in debt.*

The effect of the benefit tapers described in Figures 4.1 to 4.3 is a final income which varies marginally with earnings. On the median rate of pay – £3.66 per hour – a lone parent earning £80 each week has a final income within £5 of one earning £150. Lone mothers familiar with the world of in-work benefits did not need to understand the withdrawal rates to know that any job of 16 hours or more each week and which made them eligible for Family Credit would secure a final income little different from any other.

> *It doesn't really matter. 'Cos if I'm part-time, I can cover it up with Family Credit. So it doesn't really matter what the money were like. I'd still get Family Credit on top to cover what I'm spending anyway.* [Jenny]

> *The money I'd get doesn't really come into it because no matter how much I get it's made up with Family Credit. So it doesn't really matter how much I get.* [Elaine]

*As long as the hours suited, I'd accept any type of job really,
because I could get that Family Credit.* [Maria]

Importantly, for these mothers the extent of the financial incentive
was simply measured by comparing life on Income Support with
life on Family Credit. The typical differential is between £30 and
£45 before childcare costs are taken into account. Lone mothers
motivated by such an incentive could choose from a wider range
of job opportunities.

The more negative perspective of the final income plateau cre-
ated by in-work benefits was taken by Maureen. As a nurse, she
aspired to higher earnings and recognised that she would not have
achieved such a goal until she was clear of in-work benefit thresholds.

*If I'm still going to have to be on the benefit, then I'm not really
solving ... I'm getting to work, which solves that problem. But it's
really not going to make an awful lot of difference to how I live.*

All but a few mothers discussed financial differentials between in-
work and out-of-work incomes – even those who had no plans to
enter work. These accounts contained examples of people who felt
worse off financially in work. Fewer voiced a view that they were
better off in work, but this need not indicate that they too felt
worse off. Those who remained in work for long periods were less
likely to form part of the sampling frame. The workers in the
sample might feel less need to comment on their comparative welfare if they felt it self-evident, perhaps because they were less sure
of the comparison, or simply because they felt less need to justify
their position and decision to work in financial terms.

While the awareness of a financial incentive to work obviously
mattered to these lone mothers, it was not the whole story. A comparison of the accounts they gave suggested that similar levels of
monetary gain were perceived in different ways, and that some
mothers would continue in work even if they felt little better off,
where others would not contemplate going to work without the
certainty of a large reward. Still others, possibly the majority of
those out of work, had little opportunity to compare different situations in work and merely guessed at hypothetical in-work
incomes. Without a knowledge of the benefit structure, they

expressed a fear of the unknown. As lone mothers of young children they had perhaps too much to lose to risk an uncertain gain.

THE COST OF CHILDCARE

Topic guides were constructed and interviewers briefed to avoid
introducing discussion of childcare costs until the second half of
interviews. This gave the best chance of weighing the importance
of childcare against the background of other motives and barriers
to work in the minds of our respondents. When respondents were
asked about their employment and family history, and problems
they had taking up work, they were more likely to enter into a
frank discussion of the full range of problems they had encountered than if the discussion was centred on childcare. The relative
importance they placed on childcare would be seen in part by the
point at which the issue was raised by the respondent.

Along with other in-work costs, childcare costs played an
important part in Rebecca's decisions about work.

> *Is it going to be worth my while? Are they going to pay enough that
> I can pay a childminder? Like I say [older son] doesn't need a child-
> minder, but [younger son] does. Luckily there is a childminder that
> lives across the road. She takes him to school, but are you prepared
> to lose £50 or £60 out of your money to go to work? You can pay
> a childminder the same amount as you're actually going to end
> with. Sometimes you look at it and you think 'God, I'm going to be
> out 14 hours a week and half of it I'm going to be giving to some-
> one else'. 'Am I going to lose my Housing Benefit?' ... It all adds up
> in the end. And really you're looking for something ridiculous like
> £300 a week. There aren't any jobs to make it worth your while.*

Rebecca was actively seeking work, and although others, like
Marsha, were not, the childcare issue was still important. She
wanted to resume her previous work, hairdressing. In assessing
necessary earnings while paying for childcare, Marsha also ventured a £300 estimate.

Childcare problems were not restricted to low-income lone
mothers. One well-paid lone mother with a career, who earned
considerably more each week than Rebecca and Marsha's utopian
£300, also spoke of problems with paying for childcare. Sian was

unlikely ever to leave work because of the cost of childcare, but she did note its effect on her finances.

> *You're talking about over a hundred pounds a week for babies. The sacrifice you're being asked to make in leaving your child some-where that is not suitable – in order to earn very little extra a month.*

Maureen, a qualified nurse, needed childcare to cover her likely shift hours, and expected it to be expensive.

> *The biggest main problem will be childminding. The cost, on top of all the other costs, I just don't know if there's a job out there that I could do that's going to cover me. I'm not wanting to be absolutely mega rich, but I would like to be able to pay my bills and say to [my daughter] 'You want that? That's not a problem!'.*

There was some doubt as to whether the labour market could pro-vide Maureen with a job which paid sufficiently well to cover the cost of childcare. Maureen still hoped to solve the equation in favour of work, even if it meant trading down her skills. Her opti-mism was not shared by June, who felt she could not afford to work until her children entered school.

> *I wouldn't be able to afford a childminder for them. My mum wouldn't be able to have them: she's got too much to do. I wouldn't be able to afford rent. I wouldn't be able to do it. I mean, I'm just about scraping through now, but the wages people pay today...*

In these equations, neither the source of employment nor the sources of childcare are necessarily fixed and so neither are wage rates or the cost of childcare per hour. Lone mothers who were contemplating vacancies at the time of interview had to find jobs which would meet their childcare costs or adjust their childcare costs to what the job could pay.

At the time of interview Marion had just applied for a job in a nightclub and was in the process of working out what she could afford to pay for childcare.

> *What can you offer them for staying from nine till two in the morning? I couldn't offer them a fiver. I'd only be getting £3. Four*

hours on a Monday at £3.20 an hour and six hours on a Saturday, that's if I do get it, I mean I might not yet.

Meg lived in a rural area with very few potential employers. Before she was laid off in 1993, she used to get paid £84 a week for an eight hour day: £2.10 an hour. Her mother used to care for her children. Now her mother had moved away, Meg could not envisage doing similar work and paying for childcare for her two year-old. A full-time childminder would require more per hour than she would earn.

A lot of childcare runs away with most of your money. You're giving them most of your wages just to pay them because I think they're £3 an hour … it wouldn't be so bad if the baby was at school.

Another rural resident, Tanya, a never-partnered 22 year-old mother of a son aged two, worked full-time in a hotel and claimed Family Credit. She faced a similar problem to Meg in taking on more hours because she would be required to pay for childcare. Her relatives provided childcare for her part-time job, but Tanya was unwilling to pressure her relatives into covering the longer hours the promotion would require.

They've offered me senior receptionist. But I had to turn it down, 'cos I've got [my son] and I just can't afford to do the job. I'd have to pay a nanny. And I've looked into it and they cost about £4 an hour. So I'll have to wait until he goes to school.

Some were thinking about working and childcare equations in a more abstract way. May was much keener on working during school hours.

It would be expensive to pay for childcare, wouldn't it, in the evenings? Would it be worth working? I don't think evening work is that well paid: bar work, and waitressing.

In these examples it is not the simple cost of childcare which is a problem, it is its affordability. Acceptable, paid-for childcare comes at a price which the wage rates of better-paid jobs cover, but which could be unaffordable at lower rates at pay. Likewise, some jobs require hours of work for which care is more expensive than others. Childcare with the same fixed cost, or cost per hour, could be affordable in the context of one job opportunity and unaffordable in the context of another. Mothers also had different notions of what constituted acceptable care. The *affordability* of *acceptable* childcare could thus be an issue for mothers with widely varying earning potentials.

Quite clearly there were women for whom childcare cost was not an issue. They had free care available from friends or family, often their mothers. If these women were motivated to work, they were either in work or held back by other in-work costs: childcare costs were not the major barrier. As the previous chapter showed, some with free care nonetheless preferred their traditional roles of child-rearer and homemaker. Some with similarly little motive to work would also have faced paying for childcare in work of 16 hours or more: childcare costs once again were not the barrier.

Other women out of work or in work contemplating working more hours who would have to pay for care were attempting to solve the simultaneous equations of finding a job whose hours and wage rate made a suitable childcare source viable. Some would need to match the final income against other in-work costs from which childcare costs were inseparable. Nonetheless a subgroup of one fifth of interviewees emerged for whom childcare costs were the only substantial barrier to work entry. If childcare were cheaper they would either be looking for work, or be in work of 16 hours or more each week.

THE CHILDCARE DISREGARD

Lone parents' comments on the introduction of the childcare disregard are presented in Chapter Eight. It is sufficient here to concentrate on how it changed lone parents' perceptions of the financial incentive to take up work.

While most lone parents were aware of the disregard, not all were clear about how it worked for it to alter their perceptions of financial incentives sufficiently. Others were quite sure that it would not apply to them, either because their children were too old or because they had no plans to pay for formal childcare. Several, like Elaine and Sonia, had a clear idea of how the disregard would work. Parents who had used formal childcare in the past, like Elaine, saw the disregard as helpful, if a little late to meet their needs.

> *Now if you're on Family Credit, you can actually claim £40 a week. Whereas when I was looking for somebody you didn't actually get any help for the childminder.*

Some took exception to the requirement for a childminder to be registered to qualify for the disregard. Sonia assumed that it was up to the claimant to register their childminder, and that this would add to the start-up costs of entering work.

> *The person looking after him would have to be registered, and that's £10. So somebody's got to pay that. Then you have to fill in a claim form to claim childcare, and then I think that goes on top of your Family Credit book weekly and then that would be down to you to give to the childminder.*

As highlighted at the beginning of this chapter, some parents will see no more Family Credit as a result of the disregard but will pay less rent. It was argued that parents might find it difficult to disentangle the incentive effects of the disregard from the mechanics of the claiming process. Eileen did her best to describe how the childcare disregard affected her rent rebate.

> *I had to pay like, £65 Housing Benefit not taking into account the £25 I had to pay [for childcare] so instead of paying £50 towards me [rent] I only had £25 to pay towards it. 'Cos you didn't actually, like get [childcare] paid for plus your Housing Benefit.*

Steph had decided to work full-time as she faced similar childcare costs with any part-time job she took. Her registered childminder had advised her to apply for Family Credit. Consequently, she viewed the whole benefit as help with childcare.

> *[The childminder] had said to me to apply for Family Credit. She said to me 'It won't be very much, but it will help towards your childcare costs'. And that's what I see Family Credit as: as a help towards your childcare costs. I didn't see Family Credit as being something else. Is it something else?*

Steph was very low paid. Her full-time job as a legal secretary earned her less than £100 each week. She received maximum Family Credit, so the net result of the disregard was the difference between maximum Family Credit and what she would have received if she did not pay for childcare: about £13. If her childcare costs were to rise, her next Family Credit claim would not rise accordingly.

In situations where the childcare disregard applied, it would undoubtedly have made paid work, which relied on paid formal childcare, more attractive financially. That Steph was not aware of how much more she received as a result of its introduction did not make the disregard any less effective in producing a final income from earnings and Family Credit she felt able to live on.

THE SCENARIOS

This chapter has concentrated so far on lone parents' discussions of their experiences in and out of work. It has also explored how those more distant from the labour market view the difference taking up work together with in-work benefits could make to their final incomes. But lone parents have very different impressions of what work has to offer, and some have poor knowledge of their entitlement to in-work benefits. In interpreting outcomes it is difficult to separate pessimistic expectations of wage rates from high estimates of in-work costs or poor knowledge of the benefit system. It is one thing to talk hypothetically about the cost of childcare. It is another to state what childcare accepting a particular job opportunity might require and whether it can be afforded from the wages. This problem was tackled in interviews by presenting respondents with two potential job vacancies or scenarios.

Respondents not already working 16 or more hours each week were presented with two cards and asked how willing they would be to take each job if it were available immediately ('next week'). They were also asked their childcare intentions were they to take the job. Both jobs required the lone mother to work from nine to five, to ensure that childcare was required for at least some of the working day. The scenarios are presented in the box.

Job A paid £3.20 per hour – a little under the median for lone parents in employment – while Job B paid over twice as much, £7.14 per hour, before tax and deductions.

JOB SCENARIOS

Job A

Company	Ceramic giftware manufacturer
Job title	Packer
Job description	Packing specialist gift items for distribution to retailers
Hours	9am - 5pm Mon–Fri
Gross pay	£112 per week

Job B

Company	Japanese micro-electronic company
Job title	Micro-electronic fitter
Job description	Assemble parts and sub-assemblies using hand and machine tools (initial 4 weeks on-site training)
Hours	9.00 - 5.00 Mon–Fri
Gross pay	£220 per week while training £250 per week thereafter

Accepting Job A would nearly always make the parent eligible for Family Credit. The net income for the model lone parent described in Figures 4.1 to 4.3 were she to have Job A or Job B is given in Table 4.3

Lone parents with free childcare would be about £40 better off in Job A, and just under £100 better off in Job B than they would be out of work. These differentials were reduced if they paid for childcare, to about £35 and £60 respectively. A lone parent with two children only just qualifies for Family Credit with Job B, and then only if she pays for childcare. She gets £2.26 per week. With one child, she does not qualify. It is worth noting that there is less than £20 difference in final income between the two jobs for a lone parent who pays for childcare and receives the childcare disregard. For each job the respondent said she was willing to do, a discussion followed on childcare needs. Reasons for turning down either of the vacancies were also explored.

Table 4.3   Net final income for 'model' lone parent in receipt of all
benefit entitlements: out of work and in scenario jobs

	with one child aged 0–10	with two children aged 0–10
Out of work	120.28	135.93
In Job A		
paying for childcare		
without childcare disregard	120.98	137.96
with childcare disregard	155.48	171.70
with free childcare	160.98	177.96
In Job B		
paying for childcare		
without childcare disregard	180.10	188.35
with childcare disregard	180.10	190.61
with free childcare	220.10	228.35

Model lone parent pays £37.50 rent, £6.28 Council Tax, and receives £10 maintenance each week. When in work and paying for childcare, she uses £40 worth of formal childcare each week.

We were particularly interested in how essential it would be for lone mothers to pay for childcare in order to undertake the hypothesised jobs. If they would be willing to take both jobs, the intended source of childcare might nevertheless differ due to the different wages offered. Respondents were encouraged to explain how they decided how much they could afford to spend on childcare.

The job scenarios were constructed to present lone parents with vacancies which they might realistically apply for, thus generating a need for childcare. The more generous wage rates for Job B served to encourage those who had discussed their work decisions in the context of their previous experience of low wage rates, or who simply had low expectations of the financial returns from work.

As interviewers needed to discuss childcare in the context of in-work situations which nearly all parents would consider and would require childcare, the wage rates had to be sufficiently attractive, even in the absence of knowledge about possible in-work benefit top-ups. If parents rejected both job vacancies, there would be no work scenario to focus on. Pay rates for Job B were thus plausible but quite generous.

As intended, the scenarios did in practice encourage discussion of work entry among those who had stated they had no intention to return in the near future. Eileen was one who was determined to stay out of work.

> *I'm hoping to go back when [my son] starts school. I'm not going to look for a job until he's started school. I think [my son]'ll go when he's four. So it'll be two and a half years off.*

[Interviewer: And you want to stay at home until then?]

> *I'm determined now. I've tried it and it didn't work so.*

On presentation of the Job B card, Eileen's position changed.

> *I probably would be tempted, but I don't know whether it would work, like with [my son], but like for a pay like that I would be tempted to give it a try.*

[Interviewer: But what about the first one? The packer.]

> *No, I don't think so. 'Cos I wouldn't be any better off with that one. With the second one I definitely would.*

In this way interviewers could discuss with respondents their childcare arrangements for a concrete job opportunity, one they would be likely to take up in their current circumstances. Perhaps more important for the study question, reactions to scenario cards revealed that respondents' considered and apparently final positions on work entry were not so final. Statements that the respondent would not return to work, or could not consider using childcare, were made in the context of their perceptions of what the labour market had to offer. In the context of available jobs which paid well – enough in many cases to lift the respondent out of the reach of means-tested benefits – respondents' positions changed.

Such a finding is obviously important to the debate about work entry. Many out-of-work lone parents who currently reject the idea of working could consider employment if they were offered better-paid vacancies. Such jobs evidently do offer some incentive.

But is it the crude wage rate which is important? Clearly it is all the respondents have to go on in considering an advertised vacan-

cy or one of the study's scenario cards. But Tables 4.1 to 4.3 show
that in practice, once benefit entitlements and tax deductions have
been taken into account, the wage rate is not a good predictor of
final income. The differential in final income between the less
well-paid job and the better-paid is not the £138 the wage rate
implies but more like £25 or £19. So if the respondent would be
happy with a final income of £191 from Job B, would they not
also consider a final income of £172 from Job A? The question
was not put to respondents in such terms because the differentials
would vary from family to family. But it seems likely that were the
final income from a lesser-paid job seen to be much closer to that
from a better-paid job than the crude wage rate implies, respondents would be more likely to consider work entry even in the
context of less well paid jobs. The issue then becomes less the
actual pay differential between current employment circumstances
and 'well-paid' job scenarios, and more respondents' perceptions
of how the benefit and tax systems work to produce more similar
final incomes. The following accounts show how respondents'
knowledge and views of the effect of tax and benefit on their final
income differed. The role played by these differing perceptions
will be returned to later.

Job A was presented first. Meg was alone in her view that Job
A was well-paid.

> *That's quite good actually.*

Most respondents felt the wage to be on the low side, but not so
low as to reject the job out of hand. Some entered into quite
detailed calculations before they would give interviewers their
verdict.

> *Nine to five is brilliant for me, but the money is no good. If I get
> £112, what is it I'm left with? I don't know whether they're still
> going to pay my rent. I don't know whether they're still going to
> pay the school meals for my children, if they're still going to get
> uniform grant for the children. And then I've got to think of the
> transportation and light bills so... [Julie]*

> *Cheapest childminder that I know is £1.50 an hour, so if that's 40
> hours, supposedly. So that's going to set you back [calculates] £50,
> that's going to take £50 out. If you've got stoppages out of £112*

that's going to leave you £62 if that was your whole lot. But it's going to be less than that, so it's going to leave you probably about £50. If you earn £112 a week I doubt very much whether you'd get full rent rebate. I think you'd have to pay some rent, some more council tax. Fair comment you'd probably get a bit of Family Credit on that, but it wouldn't be an awful lot. And if you've got Family Credit I'm sure it must take your income up and over the bracket for getting benefits and things: Housing Benefits. There's nothing else you can get, if you've got that you couldn't get free school meals for a start. [Rebecca]

I can earn £140 and get Family Credit, so I'd get a fair whack of Family Credit, but not an awful lot. [Maureen]

The principal concern of a number of respondents was whether the net income would exceed the weekly amount of their current Income Support. Rachel thought so, but May doubted it would.

It's not bad, is it? £112. I'd take it, because it's better than what I'm getting now. [Rachel]

It probably wouldn't cover me Income Support. [May]

The verdict among out-of-work lone parents was mixed. Some would accept the job while others would not. Those who rejected the job gave reasons which centred on their perceptions of their final income on Job A as too low. Esther, 38, had no qualifications. Despite this, she offered up a diverse curriculum vitae including telephonist, marketing secretary, photographer, air stewardess, manager of a computer consultancy and psychogeriatric carer. She was separated from a cohabitation and was six months pregnant at the time of interview. To undertake Job A now, she would need care for her 7 year-old daughter.

No because I'm looking at £70 a week childcare. I would gross on £112 a week, about £69 after tax and insurance, so absolutely not. I wouldn't even earn enough to get me there and get me home. [Esther]

I get a rent rebate now. I'd have to pay rent if I went back to work full-time, and community charge, the full of it. Not on that amount of money. [Jackie]

What is important at this stage is that job vacancies were not rejected out of hand. No respondent said at this stage in the interview that they were not in a position to consider any work at the present time. The debate focused on the financial gains and losses associated with the job rather than the hours or tasks *per se*. Jenny was insistent that she wanted to spend more time with her son, but most others simply embraced the need for childcare within their financial deliberations and decisions to accept or reject.

I'd rather have three o'clock. 'Cos I'd have some time to spend with [my son].

This is not to argue that parents were willing to give up time with their children. (The scenarios had been designed to ensure that some childcare would be required.) For parents who had spoken of how work would interfere with the time they had to spend with their children, the financial return from work had to be sufficient to justify the loss of family time together. If respondents did not feel it was, they rejected the job. Thus Janet rejected Job A, and in so doing all full-time work.

Because of the children's ages, I still think I should be here for them, and the other reason: financially, I'd be worse off ... Yes I'd increase my hours but there's no way I'd work full-time.

But she changed her orientation to her need to be with her children, and thus to full-time work when presented with Job B.

But then you're talking about £1,000 a month aren't you, so with tax relief and that, yes. I would consider that more.

Although the job scenarios were designed with the same number of hours, perceptions of the need for different types of childcare did change between Job A and Job B. This reflected respondents' ability to afford different types of childcare under different scenarios. Maxine, for example, would have accepted either job, but would use her mother to care for her two children with Job A but a nursery with Job B.

More subtly, the attractiveness of Job B made mothers more willing to consider taking up work. The extent of the *mental* search for childcare could be widened when work was more attractive. Esther calculated the cost of childcare for Job A to be £70 (see above). For Job B, however, she describes childcare costing half as much.

> *I think she charges £1.75 an hour and that would be four hours, I think it works out about £25 a week, so that's £35 a week.*

Such a turnaround illustrates the childcare cost dilemma well. Esther gives the cost of childcare as her main reason for rejecting Job A. But in accepting Job B, she will use childcare which costs half as much. What is the true barrier to work entry here? It is not childcare cost but the attractiveness of the job vacancy. This is not to say that Esther is distorting her reasons to suit her circumstances. In the next chapter, respondents describe how the expected cost and availability of childcare does indeed vary with the particular vacancy. Where relatives or children provide the care, they may be more willing to do so, or to do so at lower cost, where they perceive the net benefits to the lone mother as more worthwhile. Thus care may be offered only for the mother to take up what is perceived to be a 'good' job.

When Esther elaborated on her position, it became clear that other lone mothers in her block would be supportive of her returning to work in a 'good' job, to the extent of offering childcare for her daughter.

> *If I was earning that kind of money what I could probably do would be to persuade one of my friends to take the children one or two days a week for a lot less than I would pay a childminder and then pay a childminder for the rest. That would give me two things, a) it would give me work and b) it would give us possibly just a little bit more money to play with.*

Job scenarios were constructed to be plausible and attainable. No respondent should have felt either job out of her reach. For the purposes of the job scenario exercise, the relative attractiveness of each job was intended to rest largely on the rate of pay. Esther was the only respondent to prioritise attributes of the vacancy other than the wage rates, hours or the tasks involved. She was particularly keen to emphasise how the characteristics of employer B would match her own needs as a lone mother out of the labour market for some time. Her detailed reasoning is worth repeating here as it demonstrates the additional attractiveness to her of Job B.

My main reason for taking this job would be the company. a) It's Japanese which means it's got money. It's not going to fold. It's micro-electronics which means its what everybody's using and doing at the moment, so there is possibility to move. There would be in-house jobs that would be better than the job they're in now and I would be able to do them. So yes, I would give that a chance. Because I feel that there would be somewhere for me to get promoted and earn more money. Plus the Japanese are very child-orientated and they are aware that their female workers have children because they mainly employ females on the shop floor. And a lot of Japanese companies have crèches and if they don't have crèches they can usually be persuaded into having one.

Emma also talked of the added impetus a well-paid job vacancy could have on her childcare search.

You'd maybe try that wee bit harder to get somebody.

More generally, nearly all out-of-work lone parents were prepared to consider work entry for Job B.

Yeah. Because you'd need that kind of money to run a house and get somebody to look after the children as well. Nine to five's not so bad. I could get somebody to take them to school, and probably get me mum to pick them up. [Elizabeth]

I could probably scrape by on that. No benefits whatsoever on that. Be worth a go. [Maureen]

Most respondents knew that Family Credit would play some form of top-up role, but were not certain of how significant this role would be. Job B was thus perceived to present a better return than Job A in most cases. Alison was one of four respondents who thought that the lack of Family Credit or Housing Benefit if they took up Job B would actually leave them worse off financially than if they took up Job A.

> *I usually stick in one bracket, the same kind of bracket. 'Cos it's easier, with my Family Credit. I'm reluctant to go for a higher-paid job. 'Cos I think, well, I'll just lose out on my Family Credit.*

Alison perceived her marginal tax rate to be greater than 100 per cent, and this discouraged her from seeking better paid work. Rebecca too was doubtful that after the loss of passported benefits with Income Support or Family Credit, she would be better off with Job B.

> *If you saw that and that in the Jobcentre you'd immediately think: 'Good God £250 for that and £112 for that'. You'd go for that, but if you sat down and actually thought about it and went through everything you're entitled to and how much time you'd spend away from home and away from your children and things, then it's not quite as attractive as it first looks ... school meals would then set you back nearly £6 a week. You wouldn't have enough to live on.* [Rebecca]

> *It wouldn't be worth me working for that amount of money with the things I have to pay out now. I'd have to pay Community Charge. I'd have to pay me rent. I'd have to pay for me dental, prescriptions, school dinners, a couple of others ... Because then I wouldn't get Family Credit for that one ... Well I suppose about five pound a week.* [Marsha]

Thus the introduction of job scenario cards allows an insight into how lone parents perceive the labour market and how the benefit and tax systems interact to make particular job opportunities seem beneficial or worthwhile. It is clear that parents do not have perfect knowledge of the latter, and that the context in which decisions about whether or not to work are made is typified more by jobs of type A than type B.

Presentation of job scenarios which respondents might accept provided a context in which the availability of childcare and its cost could be constructively addressed with those out of work. The rest of this chapter examines one particularly expensive period of childcare use – during holidays – concentrating on anticipated childcare costs perceived for a nine to five job by the out of work, and by those in work who refer to their current arrangements.

THE COST OF HOLIDAY CHILDCARE

Analysis of PSI/DSS survey data in Chapter 2 has shown that childcare costs rise during school holidays for a substantial number of parents in work. Parents of school-age children who normally rely on school to provide a free source of childcare may find themselves paying for up to 30 hours or more of additional care. In addition, some school-based sources of care, after school schemes, nursery schools and crèches, may not be available outside of school terms, or may cost more. Among those out of work, it may be the anticipated cost or availability of care specifically during the holidays which acts as a disincentive on work entry.

Rebecca was one parent who gave the cost of care during holidays as one reason why she was not working.

> *During school time would not be a problem because you'd obviously only pay a childminder probably on an hour in the morning, couple of hours at night. That wouldn't be too bad. But come school holidays if you've got to put them in with a childminder full-time, that's when the money would go down.*

A further problem with childcare availability could be that childminders are unwilling to take on children for holiday time only. Childminders with a limited number of places might prefer to take children – perhaps only pre-school age – from those parents who need childcare all year round.

> *I think a lot of them aren't so struck on parents who just want them during the holidays, because it doesn't pay.* [May]

Parents in work had to solve the problem of holiday care. Those who were unable to solve the problem are unlikely to have been found in work. However, not all in our sample had yet solved the problem since workers in the sample were chosen who were recent work entrants. For some, like Carrie, the resolution was far from satisfactory. She had solved the problem in the past by deliberately leaving work when school holidays began. She considered this less of an option now that she had secured a better job.

> *The six weeks holiday. I haven't got a babysitter. So I've got to pay somebody. So then I will literally be working to be worse off than on Income Support. But what I used to do, I'll be honest, when she was younger, I used to deliberately pack a job in when the summer holidays were coming. And then get another job. But this job, I can't do it, 'cos it doesn't work like that. It's not a little casual job. So I will be worse off, for six weeks.*

For Carrie, availability of childcare posed the major difficulty. Others like Sue saw holidays as a problem, but through drawing on a network of different sources of care including her own, she was able to continue working.

> *That's a problem [laughs], I take some time off, her father takes some time off. His mother looks after her for a little while, or my dad or friends. Childminder every so often.*

Understandably, accounts of very high childcare costs during holidays were rare. The cost differential is a problem which affects parents of school age children only, and then only those who are at least prepared to contemplate term-time costs. Those liable to pay high costs during holidays either must budget effectively so that term-time savings provide additional holiday-time funds, or avoid the need for holiday care: taking work during term-time only, or staying out of the labour market.

SUMMARY

The benefit system is structured to offer some level of financial incentive for each additional hour worked by lone parents. It is also designed to offer parents a considerably higher income in work than out of work. But not all lone parents see the system in this way. Although they want more money their knowledge of how the benefit system interacts with potential wages is imperfect. A few have large mortgages which makes a move from Income Support to paid work doubly difficult even before childcare is taken into account. They are also clearer about their position regarding help with housing costs when they are in work. Others are concerned about the effect of other in-work costs on their final income. Foremost among these costs are those for childcare, though realistically these are rarely considered alone. Travel costs, clothes, school meals all feature together with childcare. Although a new in-work benefit disregard covers some of the childcare costs, knowledge of how this might work was once again uncertain.

Use of 'job scenario cards' among those out of work showed that good wages can transform lone parents' thinking about this issue. Paradoxically, their reasoning seemed more closely tied to the crude wage rate than likely final income in work even though they were aware of Family Credit and the childcare disregard. Problems with childcare cost and availability faded in sight of the more financially attractive of the two jobs, although a small number saw net financial losses from any job which did not attract means-tested supplements. Paying for holiday care presented an additional disincentive for a minority.

Notes

1   This figure closely matches the median reservation wage rate (£3.75 per hour) quoted by lone parents not working 16 hours or more each week at the time of the National Survey – among those prepared to state an amount.

2   The median cost of childcare per hour worked by members of our 1994 sample (and who paid for term-time childcare) was £0.88. The median hourly payment for those who used and paid for only professional childcare was £1.04.

3   From April 1996, childcare costs of up to £60 each week are allowable. Since the model lone parent pays £0.88 per hour, she does not fully exhaust the £40 disregard, let alone the £60 one, even when working 40 hours each week. Thus, as far as the modelled case is concerned, the increase in allowable childcare costs has no affect on her budget constraint. The 1994/95 benefit rates are used here since these represent the system effective at the time of the study.

Chapter 5

PREFERENCES FOR WHO CARES
FOR CHILDREN

Lone parents' access to paid work is not only the outcome of the equation of motive and incentive versus childcare opportunities and cost we have explored so far. Lone parents have strong preferences about the suitability, even the legitimacy of one kind of childcare over another. Childcare which is unacceptable is unlikely to be used regardless of its cost, and other types may be tolerated only for short periods. Similarly, parents and children may see some forms of care as desirable, a suitable complement or supplement to parental care. These types of care may be sought for reasons other than their coverage of work hours. Parents may work in part to pay for their preferred form of childcare. Either way, feelings about the available sources of care will influence the hours of work and the acceptability of different rates of pay in work.

Many factors, legal status, media interest, social and private discourse, experience and prejudice, will influence parents' decisions about what constitutes good care. Such factors will also define which sources are drawn upon and, in turn, which are made available. A considerable literature has focused on the benefits and disadvantages of separating parents and their children and on different forms of care provision (notably Bowlby, 1964 on the deleterious effects of separation; Clarke-Stewart, 1980 and others reviewed in Mayall and Petrie, 1983). This study does not intend to add to this discussion, but professional scepticism about the value and quality of childcare may influence mothers' choices about the use of childcare.

Parents of children with special needs may be even less flexible in their choices of suitable care. Sources of childcare may need to be more specialised – and more expensive – or required for longer periods of the child's life, extending into teenage and beyond. Children with behavioural difficulties may be more likely to reject certain or all types of care.

It is important that the views of children are not overlooked. Children's acceptance and rejection of different forms of care, and of *any* separation from their parents, will be influential in the types of care used. Children may even choose their carer and thus be influential in determining the cost of childcare. Children's views on the childcare they use have been elicited by Smith (1995). She found some seven in ten users of holiday play schemes aged more than seven years felt the decision to use the scheme was their own.

Older children's discussions with their parents will also play an influential role in how parents perceive the effect of separation and the use of childcare. A full analysis must include not only parents' perceptions of their children's needs, but also children's perceptions of their parents' needs.

> *I was going out last night, and I says to her, 'D'you mind me going out?' She said, 'No, you've got to have a life'. She's only ten!* [Carrie]

PARENTAL CONTACT WITH CHILDREN

The primary determinant of the use of childcare will be the willingness of parent and child to spend some (additional) time apart. The care provided by the lone mother herself will always represent the baseline source of care against which other forms are alternatives. Parental care will also be the yardstick against which other care is judged. Parents may be unwilling or unable to identify weaknesses in the care they offer their child, and may find it difficult to identify reasons which justify an alternative.

Until the point when the use of childcare for pre-school children is contemplated by parents for the first time, children and parents will have spent little time apart. This will apply especially in the case of never-partnered parents who rarely had the option of leaving the children with their father. Separation will represent a new and perhaps threatening experience for both mothers and children. Parents may anticipate their children's anxiety at being placed in such a situation.

> *I just like mine to know who they are staying with. I would like them to feel sort of secure in the surroundings, not sitting there biting their fingers waiting for their mum to come home.* [Joanna]

Alternatively, satisfying the continual demands of children may in itself pose a threat to the parent – particularly for a parent who feels she has insufficient resources to do so. Others may thus have more mixed views about separation. Their worries are tempered by the temporary suspension of their parental responsibilities.

> *I think everybody needs a break from everybody. I mean if you're there with them 24 hours a day you get on top of each other all the time.* [Elaine]

> *That's a lovely feeling when you walk out the door, because you never have to listen to it. I worry about them all night.* [Cynth]

Maria felt that separation could even improve the quality of the parenting she offered in the intervening time. An alternative carer could also offer an alternative stimulus for her child.

> *If I had a job it'd be some outside interest as well. Gives us both a break from each other. Then you wouldn't get like so ratty with her. 'Cos it's constantly there, she's there all the time now and demanding me all the time, 'cos there's nobody else. If I could get a job and get out it'd give us both a break. 'Cos she could benefit from seeing somebody else as well.*

The academic debate on the effects of 'maternal deprivation' and on the benefits of exposure to other adult and educational stimuli early in childhood continues, and it is not possible for a report such as this to contribute to the debate. We can nonetheless document the behavioural consequences of childcare use reported by mothers. Parents tended to attribute children who had been placed in childcare early with greater independence and less parental attachment compared with children who had stayed at home. If a stronger attachment to parental care does indeed develop over time among children who stay at home, this might make more problematic the parent's separation from the child and the use of childcare later in the child's life.

> *He was six months old and it was heart rending but I had no choice but to do it. Fingers crossed, I was very lucky. He turned out to be a very well balanced child, but I saw other kids the same age as him who started at day nurseries same situation – because we had no choice but to go out to work – and they turned out to be very insecure little children. That's not a guideline to go by 'cos like [my daughter] she stayed at home until she was five and I couldn't have devoted more attention to any child than I did to her and she's like a blinking leech she really is, she doesn't let me go anywhere.* [Sharon]

> *She's very clingy. Makes me feel a bit guilty. But then again, she's been living at home all the time.* [Steph]

Sophie's son had been visiting a childminder for eight years.

> *He's now very independent. For ten, he is a very independent little boy. He's not clinging to me. He mixes well with other kids, mixes well with adults.*

One of the ways in which children could gain from separation was through exposure to different forms of care. Parents were provided with some post facto rationalisation for their decision to use childcare. Tracy felt that her childminder was able to contribute to her child's development in a way for which she lacked the patience.

> *She sits and plays with them and makes games and things, whereas I've got no patience that way.*

Several mothers felt that using childcare improved their children's social skills.

> *She probably gets on better with children having been around other children a lot more as opposed to being on her own.* [Sue]

Because she's living with an adult she mixes with adults. We live in a flat with no garden. So it seemed even more important that she was with children her own age. [Judith]

They start growing up themselves, and they're independent and it sort of gives them independence really. I've found in the past anyway as soon as I've started work, I realise a change. They didn't sort of cling to me as much. Even though we're still really close all of us, there's something there now where they're more independent. It's better actually and we're probably closer because of it. [Elaine]

These benefits of the childcare itself would be important for lone parent families since there is no second adult to offer care and because they tend to have smaller family sizes.

Children's contribution to the decision to use childcare

The role of children in the decision about whether or not to use care was evident in the way May discussed her decision to stay at home. The preferences of her seven and eight year-old children were significant.

If I'd have gone to work when they were little, I think it would be easier now. Because I've never gone out to full-time work while they've been around, they're used to me being here, and they hate the idea. You know, we've sort of – tentatively discussed – if I went to work, and they had a childminder and stuff. And they absolutely hate the idea. Whereas if I'd started when they were little, they wouldn't know any different. [May]

I wouldn't now, because we've got too set in our ways. But if [my daughter] was younger, and brought up that way, then I would. But not now; she's too old to start going with childminders, and learning that kind of way. If I had a new-born now, I'd consider it for the new-born. 'Cos I think, what they're brought up, they don't know any different. [Carrie]

Thus one major obstacle for May and Carrie working longer hours was their children's reluctance to stay with a childminder. They felt that if they had returned to work earlier, they would not face such reluctance now.

Sandra speculated that her son's tendency to temper tantrums and his expectation of getting his own way might not have developed if she had been able to use a professional carer at an earlier age and he had been less familiar with the people he saw each day.

I don't know whether if I'd done that right at the start it could have been different.

Near universal separation occurs around age five years, when full-time education becomes compulsory. Children may realise that they have to go to school but nonetheless spend many early days fearful that their mother will not return to collect them. Fear of separation may be heightened for children in families where one parent has already (apparently) abandoned them.

Inferring from the evidence of these mothers, the transition to school will prove particularly difficult for those children who have not been separated from their mothers before. No doubt the compulsory and universal nature of the transition to school makes it easier for parents to justify than the transition to using childcare. They were not solely responsible for the decision to send their children to school in the same way that they would be for a decision to use childcare. Parents could also be much more confident of its educational benefits.

The education system provides a regulated and familiar environment – with established channels for redress in the event of complaint – in which mothers like June could place considerable trust. This contrasted with other environments in which they could place their children, about which they knew little.

I'd rather them be at school, being taught, rather than somebody else having to look after them. [June]

If the job was worth doing, and it was worth me going to work, and giving up benefits, and doing everything like that, I think it would be worth asking the headmistress, if my children could stay there, for a half-hour. Rather than have a babysitter that I'm going to have to pay but my kids probably don't like. [Janine]

Spending considerable time apart from children was generally seen by parents as a sacrifice which was sometimes justified by the returns from working, and sometimes not. The determinant of whether the parent thought separation worthwhile was the balance between gains and losses. The children might gain or lose from their childcare, and the parent might gain or lose from being able to work. Alison had reached a point where she felt the balance no longer favoured separation.

> *I think to myself, I'm out six days a week, working, non-stop, full-time. I'm always on the go, I never get a chance, I miss out having time with [my daughter]. And I think, what's it for? what's it all for? I think, am I wasting my time?*

The children's reaction to care was influential at all ages, since the transition to using care could be traumatic regardless of the child's age. It may be physically easier to enact when the child is younger, but not necessarily emotionally so. It may be no comfort to the mother whose child is distressed each time they separate to know that some long-term benefits are likely, and that the trauma may diminish with time.

> *When I was just going out the door to go to work, she would grab my leg and start screaming. But that lasted about two months and since then she's been okay.* [Cathy]

> *She used to cry and that made me feel quite bad. 'What am I doing to this child? She needs me!' but she got over it. She'll get up in the morning now and she quite looks forward to it ... so she's accepted it.* [Judith]

> *It was stressful, really stressful. Paying for it was fine. It was just the rushing about, and him clinging to me when I was going and I had to sneak off. I just felt really devious and horrible.* [Eileen]

For parents who are confident about their decision to work, and in the form of childcare they have chosen, the distress experienced by their children must be upsetting. For those who are less sure about their decision or their source of childcare, the children's distress may be sufficient to curtail the venture.

> *I would [return to work] when [my son] goes to school. 'Cos he's so dependent on me now. I've tried it, and it's just not worked out. I mean I really love that job. Y'know it were the sort of job I always*

wanted to do and everything, but I couldn't do it because of [my son] ... Everywhere I left him he was just upset all the time. So that was upsetting me as well. [Eileen]

I don't suppose I'd feel that bad after a few weeks, but at first I think I'd be uncomfortable about not knowing [the childminders]. [Elizabeth]

Cynth's attempts to improve her skills by attending university were cut short by her 7 year-old son's tendency to throw tantrums when separated from his mother. The family doctor advised her to give up university.

The only thing he wanted was for me to take him to school and he wanted me to be there when he finished school and that was what he wanted. So, by knocking uni on the head, it solved that problem. So he was quite happy with that.

Where children reject some form of childcare, an option remains to use an alternative source. Children with special needs, behavioural problems or who simply dislike being separated from their parents remove the option of working outside school hours altogether. Her son's tantrums meant Cynth could only work school hours.

At this point in tackling the study question another definitional problem is reached, since it is possible that children who reject separation could nonetheless be cared for by some specialised form of care. Cynth's son, after all, had been persuaded away from his mother to attend school. However, such care might be unknown to the parent or very expensive. So is the issue childcare cost or availability or is the use of childcare simply unrealistic in situations where the family cannot entertain the idea of separation?

For some mothers, the rejection of separation or of certain types of childcare are difficult to separate. Josie had been unable to persuade her daughter to attend an after-school scheme at a church, yet her daughter could give no good reason.

Now I would send her there, but she doesn't want to go ... She got christened there and she likes the people but she doesn't want to go.

It is evident that some mothers do have difficulty sending their children to the types of childcare they consider suitable. Either such sources are not available – and availability is discussed in the following chapter – or their children are not prepared to use them. The issue is further linked to how coercive parents are prepared to be, since some mothers persisted with childcare unpopular with the child and saw the child's reaction diminish with time.

If and when the separation issue has been overcome, and perhaps the entry into formal schooling does most to resolve the issue for children who stay at home to the age of five years, preferences for different types of care become important. Analysis in Chapter 2 showed that there was no clear leading preference for type among lone parents. Parents divided between those who favoured formal and those who favoured informal sources.

INFORMAL VERSUS FORMAL CARERS

The majority of parents using childcare make use of informal sources: most carers were relatives or friends. The analysis in Chapter 2 showed that those out-of-work anticipating using care were more likely to be contemplating professional sources. Non-workers may have less ready access to informal sources. One difference between workers and non-workers is thus how care is perceived and described. Workers have found childcare they consider at least tolerable, and have children who are willing to attend it. Non-workers have not only to find acceptable care, perhaps from a smaller pool of more formal carers, but to convince their children of the value of separation and of the merits of the care. Workers have had to solve the acceptability problems too, but perhaps when their children were younger or less singularly familiar with their parent's company.

The National Survey asked out-of-work parents their preferences for different forms of childcare and the sources they would never consider. No one source was favoured by a majority, but substantial minorities preferred each of parents, other relatives and registered childminders (Figure 5.1). A third indicated that they would prefer only to work school hours. The inverse relationship between preferred and unacceptable forms was as expected. Fewer than half would even consider an unregistered childminder, and only 2 per cent preferred one. Interestingly, nearly one in five would never consider using a *registered* childminder, either.

Figure 5.1   **Preferred and unacceptable forms of childcare: out-of-work lone parents**

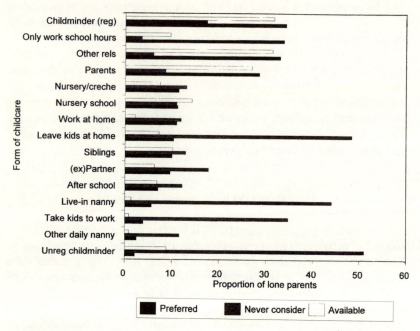

A number of factors underlie the preferences shown in Figure 5.1. No doubt children's age plays a part in determining preparedness to leave children at home or with their siblings (see Chapter 6). Cost rather than suitability may also play a role in parents' rejection of live-in help.

Respondents were also asked about the availability of each source to them: preferred sources tended to be those also most available, but many fewer thought that working only during school hours was available to them than would have preferred this arrangement. The only source where supply clearly outstripped the level of preference for it was unregistered childminders.

Parents who refused to consider any form of formal care were few and far between. In the National Survey, just 4 per cent of out-of-work lone parents rejected all formal care. Fewer still, 2 per cent, rejected all informal sources. A much stronger influence on potential use was availability, since 43 per cent said they had no informal sources available and 52 per cent no formal services. Just over a fifth felt they had access to neither. This left a fifth willing

and able to use only formal sources and a third to use only informal sources. Just under a quarter of lone parents were willing and
able to consider both categories of care.

Preference for formal care declined with age of the youngest
child, as did availability. Age of children was not related to acceptance or availability of informal sources. Sixty-one per cent had
their preferred arrangement for looking after the children available to them at the time of interview: six in ten parents whose
youngest child was pre-school age, seven in ten parents of five to
ten year-olds, but only half the parents whose youngest was aged
11 or over. The last statistic is particularly striking since preferred
arrangements could include 'leaving children at home to look after
themselves'.

These findings suggest that there is no neat division between
parents who favour formal or informal care as defined by the
availability of the disregard. A quarter favour both and a fifth have
access to neither. Some forms of informal care – such as unregistered childminders – are universally unpopular, and few parents
have available after-school or holiday schemes. There is division,
however, over the acceptability of the more available forms of formal care: registered childminders and nursery schools.

In comparing formal and informal care below, then, parents are
discussing the pros and cons of care most readily available to
them: largely the comparison is between childminders and parents
and other relatives.

For mothers who cast themselves in the role of sole child rearer,
simply contemplating the use of childcare was distressing.

*Just the thought of them crying for their mum, you know, and
someone else is shouting at them.* [June]

Limited knowledge of childcare sources, combined with hesitancy
about being apart from their children meant mothers like June
found it difficult to visualise an untroubled transition to using
childcare. Janet was asked if there were any benefits she could
foresee to using a childminder.

I've never really used one so I wouldn't really know.

Lack of knowledge did not prevent her citing disadvantages, such
as childminders' lack of discipline and their tendency to take on

too many children. She has thus constructed her own barrier to using childcare. If she cannot construct a positive picture of her children using childcare, she is unlikely to use the care. Any weighing up of the pros and cons of using care will remain one-sided.

Out-of-work parents were being asked to compare two states: their current situation and a situation where they were working and using childcare. The latter state might be one which they viewed remotely and with apprehension. The abruptness of the implied transition and implied changes in behaviour might also make it difficult for parents to view each element independently. There was certainly evidence, reviewed more thoroughly in Chapter 7 that parents approached the transition more gradually. The children of out-of-work lone parents often attend nursery school (Meltzer, 1994). Informal carers – relatives or friends – would often fulfill a wider social role within the family than just providers of care. Melanie, 23 year-old mother of three, separated from a cohabitation, and Elaine, for example, used teenage babysitters who were already firm friends of the family.

> *They know [babysitter], she's good with the kids. She's always here anyway so it wouldn't make no difference. So the only time I would look for a proper childminder is like [babysitter]'s 16 now. She's going to be looking for a job of her own.* [Melanie]

> *She's like 16, she's very capable of looking after them and I'll pay her something. It's only usually about five pound. She'll have them for the night so I can work it that way and she's always asking me 'Do I need her or this, that and the other?' so she's really reliable.* [Elaine]

For other parents, it was exactly this informality which they found unacceptable for certain forms of childcare. Sue used a registered childminder working from home to cover her work hours. She was nonetheless reluctant to use babysitters to cover evenings.

> *I don't have babysitters. If I wanted to go out one evening during the week for something it would have to be my dad or her dad, and if nobody's there I wouldn't go. I don't have babysitters into my house ... they're all quite young girls. To have somebody in your house when you go out and leave a child, I don't think it's a good idea.*

More commonly among lone parents who preferred informal sources, the preference was for childcare to come from within the family. Strong family ties, the child's familiarity with the potential carer and the care environment, flexibility and options for non-financial, reciprocal arrangements dominated the reasons.

Parents with reliable sources of family care which matched available job opportunities tended to be in work already. However, parents whose strong preference was for care within their extended family, but whose family were unable to offer such care, were more likely to be out of work.

> *If I didn't have such good childcare by my mum, then it would be difficult. I think that's probably the main factor over the last five years, why it's so easy for me.* [Sally]

> *She'd be better with one of my own family, really, if I could. Somebody who I knew. Somebody who she can relax with or she knows very well, 'cos I wouldn't have to worry about her.* [Maria]

> *Even at night time he says, 'Are we going along to Granny's?' He likes that idea. Don't think he would have it any other way either.* [Sandra]

With informal childcare sources, particularly within the family, the person lone mothers chose to look after their child could become involved more generally in the child's upbringing. The carer could become involved in some functional aspects of child rearing more commonly associated with the role of the child's other parent.

Sasha, 26, was a Family Credit claimant, separated from a cohabitation. Her mother-in-law was a childminder and looked after Sasha's 5 year-old son while she worked in a ladies' clothes shop.

> *I do involve her a lot, because his dad's not so involved. The parents' things at school. I used to take her with me. Just so she knew that she was involved in it.*

This substitution effect could extend even to the maternal role.

> *She's very close to my mum. In fact, its only recently that I actually feel as if my mum's taken over the other part ... So I say 'Mum I*

will give you a rest, I'll take her to nursery' – knowing fine well that she won't [allow it] but I just feel better. 'No, no, no, want Gran to take me'. It is actually sometimes as if it's my mum that she wants. [Sadie]

The risk of becoming more distant in their child-rearing role applied not only where carers were family members. Parents could come to resent this aspect of childcare use.

Ben said, 'I don't want you, I want to stop at Nan's' and that really hurt. [June]

I paid £1.20 a week for professional people to look after my little boy from half eight in the morning till half five at night and they did it better than I could do it. He ended up calling them 'mum' and me 'auntie'. [Sharon]

Of course, lone mothers' parents might encourage their children to seek work, and back up the encouragement through offering to care for the children. Claire took up her father's offer to go to her house to cover the evenings she spent working.

I went 'Well, it's up to you Dad, you can't turn around and say well 'no' one minute and 'yes' the next. You can't moan about it which he does. And ever since it's been great. It's been nice. It helped me anyway, not having to go over there all the time. No rush.

Illness within the extended family could restrict the range of child-care available. Janine, who held strong preferences for using child-care within her family, had run up against the high prevalence of illness in her family. The only member of her family well enough was her disabled father.

My nan's with cancer. And my other auntie, she's got leukaemia. My sister was beaten up, a few times, by her boyfriend before she got married. It carried on after the marriage. A few times, I've had to go over and stay at my sister's place. She was in hospital for a fortnight. She got a clot in her brain. My dad used to help me out during the day, but otherwise the kids wouldn't settle. [Janine]

> *I had to give up the job because my mum suffers from arthritis all over and she was minding my children ... I said 'To be honest, I don't think you are up to it' and she shouldn't have to. She's raised us, that's how I look at it. It's your turn now to sit back and enjoy the rest of what you have got, in peace.* [Claire]

Among family members, the most common preference was for the children's grandmother to offer care. Often such arrangements had built up instinctively as a consequence of lone mothers spending time with their own mothers following the child's birth, or separation from their partner.

> *I started off living with her so it was automatic anyway 'cos they lived there too.* [Sally]

> *My mum's her second mum ... If I had all the money in the world to pay for it, I'd still let her go to my mum's. 'Cos I think she gets a lot out of it, she's well looked after.* [Alison]

For some parents, their unwillingness to use formal care restricted the hours they were prepared to work. Sandra worked part-time. Longer hours would require formal carers which would increase the disruption of her own and her son's routine in a way she considered unacceptable.

> *I suppose I need to get like a full-time job, or more hours, but I don't really want that, because at least this way like my mum or my dad comes down in the morning and puts [my son] to school and I'm there going to go and pick him up again, and I'm in the house for him having his dinner, and I don't think I could, 'cos it'd be unfair to him as well. He'd be like dumped from place to place waiting on me going to get him ... She must get fed up, 'cos I think I would if that was me having to go every day. That's your morning taken up, isn't it? She's never complained yet. I'm not mentioning it!* [Sandra]

> *I'd never put it on her if it was full-time.* [Elaine]

> *Me mum has him for the hour and a quarter that I do at dinner time but I wouldn't put on her for much more.* [Margaret]

While parents were divided on the issue of whether formal carers could provide the sorts of care their families needed, some were unhappy relying on the alternative informal sources: relatives and friends. Once her daughter started at school, Sadie was no longer able to draw upon full-time formal childcare. She felt guilty relying on a combination of three relatives to take her daughter before and after school hours.

Without depending on my mum, my sister, and my mother-in-law it would just be too much. And they're not getting any younger. This morning my mum had [my daughter] twenty to eight, she walks up to the bus stop for her. To do that to her every day, to get me to work. I just don't think its fair. They've had their time of this ... I didn't mind so much when she was at that full-time nursery 'cos I felt no one was being put out. My sister came round quarter past seven yesterday morning for her to get me to work for eight and it's just not fair on people. Inconvenience to other people. It's just not practical.

Parents could feel they were imposing their needs on their family. Rebecca had rejected the offer of free care from her family.

With friends or relatives you can't do it on a regular basis. It looks as if you're taking liberties a bit – to leave with people if you're not actually paying them. When you're paying someone as a job you don't feel so badly ... they've got a definite commitment to you. It's their job to keep the service going or to provide an alternative if they can't do it. It's up to them to let you know rather than you have to chase them about. Whereas with a relative you might have to keep ringing and saying 'Is this alright?'

So parents could prefer the contractual basis of formal childcare, and the existence of recognised means of redress. Guilt could also play a part. Sian depended on her parents.

Their life is not supporting my life. They do it very happily. I'm very conscious of the fact that they're supposed to have done all that. [Sian]

I would never use my family, in that respect. Because I don't want to ever ruin the friendship. But I'd rather do things properly, and

*not have any come-back about 'Oh well, we've done that for you'.
I'm not saying that family or good friends would ever do that. But I
just wouldn't want to put on people.* [Steph]

For Ruth, the care the children's grandmother could offer was simply unsuitable.

*Theoretically I could get my mum to stay but she's 74 and bit
crotchety to say the least and I don't think they'd like it.*

Other potential sources include boyfriends, but relationships were
rarely sufficiently established for parents to feel comfortable with
such arrangements.

*I ain't been with him long. So I wouldn't really. No, I wouldn't
trust – I wouldn't leave him.* [Rachel]

*I've got a boyfriend at the moment that I've been with for about
nine months and I leave them with him if I'm just nipping to the
shops. I'm quite trusting with him. There have been other
boyfriends that I haven't known for very long and I wouldn't leave
them with them because you don't know.* [Sally]

By far the most commonly cited problem with using carers other
than friends and relatives was a fear of strangers. Almost half the
respondents specifically referred to distrust of potential sources of
care as one reason why they would have difficulty using childcare.
It is alarming how much influence media representations of child
abuse had on lone parents' preparedness to leave children with
childminders or other 'strangers'. Extracts from a number of
accounts are presented here to illustrate the extent and depth of
such feelings.

*You see it on the television, you read it in the newspapers, so I
wouldn't trust any strangers with my children. Not even someone
from an agency.* [Julie]

*Just everything you hear on telly about nannies, smacking the
children, doing things and being nasty. There's very few people I
trust with my children.* [June]

It always fears me because you see these programmes on the telly about these childminders that battered the kids and it puts me off it. Like these childminders that have sexually abused the children they've been minding, that have been registered. No, I couldn't have a registered childminder. No. [Josie]

Janice, 33, had separated from her husband, and now brought up her four year-old daughter alone.

I've heard so many things about childminders, there's lots of articles, some of them abuse them and things...

It is to be expected that parents will be protective, particularly when embarking on a new course of action. Meg described the painstaking checks she made on a childminder who was to babysit for her while she went to a party.

I was frightened. It took me about three months just to decide, because I kept asking her all these questions 'Are you sure you'll look after her?' ... I even went to see their mum and dad ... She was registered, I went down to the Social Work Department and they said that she was registered, but it took me a while.

It is difficult to predict the effect of such apprehension on the likelihood of mothers using care. After all, these mothers did not rule out friends or relatives looking after their children. Some would also accept collective care (nurseries or after-school schemes) where many children and more than one adult were present. The fear of strangers simply added a further limitation on the kinds of care the family could use. Sharon preferred collective provision to childminders.

Somewhere where lots of professional people are looking after lots of children. You don't have to worry about one particular person going a bit loopy and trying to molest your kid or anything like that because it's open.

As already noted, the range of informal sources out-of-work parents can consider is often restricted. Since childminders are often the cheapest source of more formal care, a need to seek collective provision could reduce any financial incentive associated with paid work. Some parents were constructive in their views about the childcare they would use. They tended to favour registered carers who were already known to the family. Some out-of-work parents, like Rebecca, had identified their preferred childminder, and the availability of such a known source seemed to influence strongly her willingness to use care.

> *I would use a registered childminder. I actually know someone personally. I must admit if I didn't know [childminder] across the road then that would be a different thing altogether. I wouldn't put him through an unknown childminder.*

Parents differed between those willing to accept the recommendations and certification of local authorities and others, and those who would subject the potential minder to their own initial scrutiny.

> *I'd want to see their recommendations and the forms they've got. I don't just want anybody. A proper childminder's going to be a stranger to me so I want to feel like she's going to be safe and secure there.* [Melanie]

> *I know they probably won't like it, but I will pop in, just to watch what they do.* [Jess]

> *Before I like left him with [childminder], she like invited me back to see, like how she does things and if I was comfortable with that and everything, and I said 'yeah'. So she like covered that bit for me because she was showing me what she got up to.* [Jenny]

A third group should not be ignored: those who have never considered the issue of using childcare. Jane was one of a handful for whom the issue of finding childcare was revealed as very remote when she considered each of the job scenarios in Chapter 4.

> *I'd have to find some care for them, but how to go about it? I don't know whether you'd contact the council or just look down the road in the paper shop. I should know, my father-in-law's wife is a registered childminder. But I don't know the ins and outs. How they advertise...*

Many lone parents are unfamiliar with the world of formal child-care. They have not used any formal care and neither have their friends. In the absence of their own experience, the representations of media and hearsay will hold greater sway and may influence decisions. So long as the use of childcare is rare in any network of parents' collective experiences, it is likely to seem threatening to their children's well-being and the parents' peace of mind.

Another dimension of the decision to use formal or informal care is even less clear. Formal childcare is available in discrete packages: nursery school offers collective provision with a strong educational element. School holiday schemes provide a range of set activities for children outside the home. Parents may seek care to provide security and peace of mind while they work: they may not wish for there to be any further fixed attribute to the care. Children too might not want to take part in organised activities, or might want to exercise some choice over what they do. Sian talked about her son's aversion to school holiday schemes.

> *It's this sort of forcedness that the children get fed up with. Having to go and be jolly and do organised things. I think with this adolescent lounging about. You're not allowed to do that. You have to go roller skating. With [my son], he'd like to be allowed to stay in bed until 11 o'clock tomorrow morning and he would then like to be able to lounge about.*

Should the child reject active forms of childcare, then the problem for a professional worker like Sian becomes one of availability. This issue is discussed further in Chapter 6.

It is difficult to discern what determines parents' personal preferences for formal and informal care. No doubt the strength of family ties plays a part, particularly the relationship between mothers and their daughters. Women orientated towards professional work might feel more confident using (and more able to afford) more formal sources. Mothers with more highly skilled jobs tended to favour institutionalised sources, but not exclusively so, and even Sue's childminder was a friend of a friend. What is important is the recognition that mothers hold strong views on which types of childcare are suitable and any policy needs to be flexible about the types of care taken up.

QUALITY OF CHILDCARE

Parents were asked what kinds of childcare they found acceptable, and the problems they experienced in using care. A whole range of criteria are used by parents to assess the adequacy of care. Some of the qualities discussed in interview include:

- the safety and security of the arrangement, including the child's journey to and from the care;
- the educational or social benefits it offers the child;
- the personal qualities of the carer;
- how children are controlled, disciplined or punished;
- the other adults and children the child will come into contact with as a result of using the care;
- the hours care is available for and their flexibility in line with potential changes in work hours and holidays;
- cleanliness and hygiene;
- play facilities;
- the acceptability to the child;
- the cost or, perhaps, value for money.

Available care is unlikely to excel in all aspects and parents will accept care which falls short on some or all requirements. Children will assess their care using their own range of criteria. The child's ultimate bearing on the decision to use care will be indirect: exercised largely through the parents' interpretation of their reaction. Parents were able to describe many sub-standard arrangements they had used in the past, or still used. Most often, complaints concerned the child's welfare.

> *Go into this woman's house: she had no toys. I used to leave him standing at the window just sort of standing there and when I got back there in the evening, he'd still be standing there. And I would think 'Oh God, he's been standing there all day' and that was awful because you knew that she didn't give a damn what he did and what happened.* [Sian]

Tracy's childminder seemed even less concerned about what happened to the children.

*The day I came home and found them on the steps! She'd gone away
to the town for her shopping and just left them till she came back.*

A further dilemma in the use of childcare arises from children's illness. A sick child can mean a day off work and for many jobs a loss
of pay. If the illness is serious, the parent may feel additional care is
required which only she can provide, but for minor complaints a
continuation of childcare may be more appropriate. Childcare which
continues when the child is ill will permit the parent to keep working. Families and relatives may be more likely to offer such care.
More formal carers may feel obligated, legally or professionally, to
refuse the child. In collective provision (nurseries, after-school
schemes and some childminders) the dilemma is magnified. Parents
will not want their children to mix with others who have an infec-
tious illness. At the same time, to avoid the need to find alternative
care, or to take time off work themselves, parents will want their
own children to be looked after when suffering a mild complaint.

*If [my daughter]'s not well at school, just a tummy upset, [child-
minder]'ll go and pick her up. But she's a registered childminder as
well, so I mean, they're not supposed to have them when they're ill.*
[Steph]

*Decent childcare: they won't have children if they are ill. Poor
quality childcare: they will have them anyway. Which do you
choose?* [Sian]

*They didn't like a child going there with a nasty cough because they
thought you could catch asthma, and people do protect their own
kids.* [Ruth]

A division emerged between parents who felt professional carers
could provide childcare of a sufficient quality, and those who felt
such care inappropriate in one or more respects for their own
children. For some, like Janet and Rachel, this division centred on
how well the parent knew and trusted the carer. They were not
prepared to adopt carers whose methods were not familiar.

*My mum and my friend – if they do something wrong – are allowed
to tell them off. Childminders: I don't think give the discipline and
I'm very hard to my children.* [Janet]

I don't think they'd get the attention that they need. She'd need attention. Constant watching. All the time. [Rachel]

Some parents felt children were much more likely to report bad experiences with relatives than with professionals. In another discussion of discipline, Esther described how she was only likely to get reliable feedback if the carer was on friendly terms with both herself and her daughter. Others, like Jenny, were concerned about the effects of certain types of childcare on their children's behaviour.

He's started being a bit rough. Like since he started nursery. He's changed a lot with being around the other children. Really rough sometimes.

All parents contemplating work had to weigh up whether the pursuit of one type of behaviour – working and using childcare – produced benefits which outweighed the disadvantages. Obviously physical or emotional distress among children would weigh heavily among the disadvantages. But parents like Jenny do not have the luxury of a controlled experiment. She would have to judge whether it was the childcare which brought on her son's boisterousness, or whether it would have arisen anyway, at home or when he started school.

Parents used their own experience, media representations and the experiences of their friends to judge the acceptability of care. Few parents spoke of their own observations of carers, perhaps because the remoteness of the observation prevented a sufficient insight. Emma had drawn some negative conclusions about a local childminder.

I've watched one woman in the area with some younger kids and they're always trailing behind her and ... sometimes I look and think 'Thank God that's not my toddler she's watching'. [Emma]

There were many examples of workers persisting with less than satisfactory arrangements. They may not have begun with uncertain childcare, but their arrangement may have changed over the years, or their children may simply have outgrown it.

> *It's not an ideal situation for children to be in somebody else's domestic environment ... they use language that I don't approve of, they've outgrown [their childminder] as much as she's outgrown them. She's been going there since she was five years old. She's now 11 years old. That's six years she's been going to the same place ... But she has to put up with all their domestic crises as well ... I pay £1.20 an hour for [my daughter] to be looked after by somebody who doesn't meet my full approval, if I could afford to I would certainly pay more than that. I can't really afford more than that so I make do with the £1.20 an hour.* [Sharon]

Sharon's source of childcare is tolerable. It may have been far more acceptable initially, but the children have outgrown the type of care on offer. Sharon implies that she would spend more to improve the quality of the childcare if she could afford to. Sharon has already been identified as someone highly motivated to work and she gives no indication that the poor quality of the care she can afford is making her consider giving up work. Nonetheless, the poor quality of after-school care could encourage her to seek work during school hours only. Alternatively, it may spur her on to seek better paid employment and better quality care.

That parents persist with unsatisfactory arrangements is not to say they should be prepared to enter work with childcare they find only moderately tolerable. It will be more difficult for a mother to justify a decision to enter work when it results in an instant deterioration in her children's environment, than it will be for a parent in work to observe a gradual decline in the quality of care. In the latter case, there is no new decision to justify, while the option remains to alter arrangements as soon as feasible.

Many other lone parents reported some aspect of their actual or potential childcare to be suboptimal. The frequency of problems is to be expected if childcare is viewed in some way as a substitute for maternal care. The circumstances of each family will differ, and childcare sources will vary in their ability to accommodate different types of family and replace maternal care in an acceptable way. Some parents, even a 'career' woman like Sophie, 35, earning in excess of her Family Credit threshold, felt that simply the contractual nature of the relationship would prevent suitable care being delivered.

A professional childminder is doing it for money. Not for the love of the child. Not for the sake of the child.

Maxine had more practical difficulties finding care for her two pre-school age children. She was not prepared to countenance separating them.

A lot of people say they'd do just the one. They'd have them. But I wouldn't split them up.

Religious, cultural or dietary beliefs could also create problems. Ellie was a black mother of six dependent children, separated from a cohabitation.

We're two different cultures, in respect that I'm Rastafarian, they're not. They eat different foods from my children and it causes: 'Oh I'm doing you a favour', that type of attitude, because they might be preparing separate food for my children.

For older children, the range of potential formal sources is restricted. Constant supervision is less of a necessity so that childminders become less appropriate. Also children are more likely to voice their own objections or preferences. A minority of parents knew of any formal after-school or holiday schemes in their area, and among those who did, the impression gained was negative.

You're talking about something like £30 a week and they have them from sort of half past eight till five o'clock. They have them full-time hours, but to be honest I've had such bad reports about them. Again it's parents who volunteered to go along and to look after the children and to be honest half of them can't look after their own children. [Esther]

It's a leisure centre and I've never sent the children there because I haven't liked the other children that go there. And it is for working parents because I think you can drop them off at eight or eight thirty and they have videos until nine o'clock or nine thirty when the scheme starts and then it's till four but they keep, keep care of your kids four till six after the scheme. I've never really looked into it, but they've never wanted to go to that one as a summer scheme. [Maggie]

Yet other situations existed where children were taken off their parents' hands and into suboptimal care against the parents' wishes. Cynth, for example, was required to let the children's father care for the children at weekends.

> *Leaving them with their dad? ... They don't like it, but it's a case of having to ... If I had a choice, the man would be completely out of their lives, basically, I wouldn't want nothing to do with him.*

Parents might take advantage of such arrangements to undertake paid work. They would find it easier to justify the use of suboptimal care where they were not responsible for its implementation. More often, however, unwanted care from fathers was also unreliable which made working impractical.

But what effect does such apprehension about the quality of care have on parents' willingness to consider work? Most of those wary of using childcare were out of work, and if they were considering using care it was for the first time. Some part of parents' reluctance to work could be attributed to this apprehension. Workers and those with experience of using care did report poor quality care, but the result was often a change of carer or change in the hours worked. Childminding problems rarely meant lone parents gave up work. Maureen described one of the few occasions where they did.

> *I had a childminder, but [my daughter] was one of those babies that slept all day, so I would drop her off at half past one in the afternoon and collect her at 10 o'clock at night and she hadn't been fed all day, and she was so quiet she forgot. High demand for these girls and they cost a fortune. Whatever they wanted they got.*

That those out of work foresee some problems with using childcare is to be expected. That those in work identify such problems is perhaps more worrying, but encourages the view that difficulties with childcare do not pose an insurmountable barrier to work entry. It is also important to note that childcare arrangements do not always pose problems. Not only can carers facilitate the mother's working and improve children's social and educational skills, carers can become an integral part of dynamic family life. High quality, reliable childcare can even encourage a mother to work longer hours:

My childminder's so good, the children would miss going to her! If I ever said to them 'Right, there's no [childminder] now, you're not going to [childminder]'s', they'd be really upset. In another respect, I would prefer to be doing 16 hours – two full days – and let them go to [childminder]'s. [Sarah]

The quality of childcare is a constant concern of mothers. The use of high quality care can contribute to and even improve children's development and welfare. Its availability can make parents more willing to enter work and even encourage parents to seek better paid work to pay for it. Poor quality care will deter potential job seekers and distress parents in work who use it. In the absence of alternatives the childcare issue of concern is no longer quality but availability, addressed in the following chapter. On occasion, parents who can find no alternative may be forced to quit working entirely.

SUMMARY

A common theme in this chapter has been justification. Can parents justify entering work and using childcare if it brings about a deterioration in the care their children receive? Parents must make a decision on this complex issue, most often with imperfect information. It is much more difficult to justify a decision which brings about deleterious consequences than it is to justify continuance of the status quo. Thus parents in work may be better able to continue to use care of a quality which deters potential new work entrants.

The decision parents have to justify is threefold: separating themselves and their children for substantial periods, often for the first time; placing their children in the care of another; and spending their own time in work. Each aspect of the decision will have its advantages and disadvantages. Parents with a strong orientation to child-rearing may find it more difficult to be apart from their children. Children who have been separated from one parent and spent their early years in the company of just one adult may find it difficult to be apart from that person. The value and quality of care available to each parent varies dramatically as do types of work and the amount of childcare they necessitate. Parents also hold strong and differing views about the types of care appropriate to their children.

Chapter 6

THE NEED FOR CHILDCARE AND CHILDCARE AVAILABILITY

For childcare cost or availability to act as a barrier to lone parents' attempts to work, children must need care. That children need supervision at younger ages is not at issue, but the need for care, the kinds of care suitable and acceptable to the child are likely to vary between families and the characteristics of each individual child. Parents will have their own views, based on their knowledge of their child, their beliefs about child-rearing and knowledge of accepted norms.

If a need is identified, certain types will fulfil that need. Parents will be aware of the availability of a subset of locally available care. As some potential carers are friends or relatives, there can be no objective external measurement in a study of this kind of the range of locally available childcare. But childcare will only be available to the parent who knows about it, or whose motivation to seek work and/or use care is sufficient to make her prepared to find out.

This chapter considers parents' need for care and the sorts of care they consider themselves able to draw upon. The final section uses evidence from Chapters 3–6 to identify among respondents four groups whose work intentions are differentially affected by the cost and availability of childcare. Justification is based on the broad range of factors which influence lone mothers' labour market position and their potential or actual need to use childcare. Readers will already be familiar with the groupings since these determined the convention used for respondents' pseudonyms (described in Table 1.1).

THE NEED FOR CHILDCARE

Four in ten lone parent families contain a child under school-age for whom some form of childcare is a prerequisite to taking up work outside the home. Another third contain a youngest child aged at least five but under 11 years who is likely to attend school but to require some form of care if the mother works other than school hours. The need for care at ages 11 years and older is a matter of some debate, both in policy terms – since 11 years is the cut-off point for entitlement to the childcare disregard – and among parents themselves, as the DSS/PSI National Survey and depth study reveal.

Lone parents' preferred forms of childcare are presented in Chapter 2, and their rationalisations in Chapter 5. The National Survey also asked parents not working 16 hours or more whether their child had reached an age where they would be comfortable using this preferred form of childcare. Just over one third said that their youngest child had not. They were also asked whether their youngest was old enough to be left at home without adult supervision: only 13 per cent thought so. Taking the answers to both questions together, only half the lone parents not in work of 16 hours or more had children old enough to use childcare but young enough to need it.

One substantial barrier to childcare use among those out-of-work is thus parents' feelings that their children are too young to be cared for by someone else. Fifty-four per cent of those whose youngest was aged under four years, 27 per cent whose youngest was aged five to ten, and even one in six whose youngest was aged 11 or over were reluctant to use care for a child of that age.

This reluctance to use childcare for reasons related to the child's age may have arisen in part because the question was phrased in the context of the parent's preferred form of childcare. Thus four in ten who said their child was not old enough were planning to work only during school hours – a form of 'care' not available until the child is of school-age. But a third said their child was too young for a registered childminder, and a third for relatives or friends, sources that in theory could start at any age.

The National Survey revealed a strong relationship between willingness to leave children unsupervised and age of the youngest child. Only 4 per cent of parents with youngest children aged under 11 years were prepared to consider leaving such children at

Figure 6.1   Age youngest child could use childcare: lone parents not
working 16+ hours per week

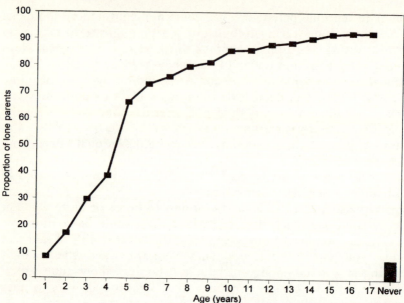

home without adult supervision. Half (54 per cent) of the parents
not working 16 hours or more each week *whose youngest child
was aged 11 years or over* felt their children old enough to look
after themselves. This still leaves four in ten parents whose
youngest was aged 11 years or older requiring childcare.

A final section of the National Survey asked all parents not
working 16 hours or more what age they would feel comfortable
leaving their youngest child in their preferred form of childcare
and at what age they would feel comfortable leaving them at home
without adult supervision. This information is presented in two
cumulative graphs in Figures 6.1 and 6.2. The convex curve in
Figure 6.1 illustrates that acceptance of using childcare rises rapidly with age for young children, but plateaus out after ages nine or
ten years. About two-thirds would be comfortable using childcare
for a five year-old and around 80 per cent by age nine years. The
mean, mode and median age was five years old. About 7 per cent
of these lone mothers would never be comfortable using childcare.
The minimum age parents felt comfortable using childcare corre-
lated fairly strongly with the age of their youngest child (r=.323,
p<.001). This implies that the younger the mother's child, the

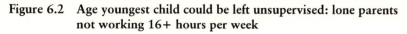

Figure 6.2   Age youngest child could be left unsupervised: lone parents not working 16+ hours per week

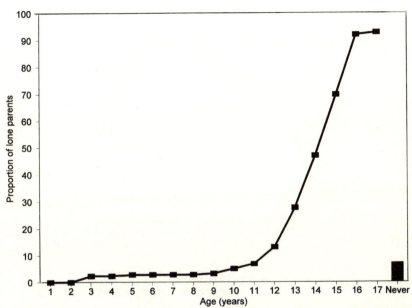

earlier she was prepared to contemplate care. It also implies that those with more experience of child rearing, whose children were older, were less likely to think childcare could be started early.

Figure 6.2 describes a concave curve, with very few parents prepared to leave a child alone before age 11 years. The majority of this small group said ten years was a suitable age, and one said nine. In all but one instance where the age quoted was under nine years of age, an older sibling was present in the households to provide care. Only one in ten were prepared to leave a child of 11 or younger alone, and fewer than three in ten a child of under 14. The mean and median age at which parents felt comfortable leaving a child unsupervised was 14, the mode was 15 and nearly all were happy with the idea once the child was 16. Once again, a small number – some with disabled children – could not contemplate leaving their child unsupervised.

Taking the answers to the two questions together it is possible to show the children's ages at which parents feel comfortable using childcare, and at which they feel childcare is necessary since they are unhappy to leave the child unsupervised. Figure 6.3 subtracts the curve in Figure 6.2 from that in Figure 6.1 and shows the peak

Figure 6.3   **Proportion of lone parents who feel childcare is needed for an unsupervised child at each age**

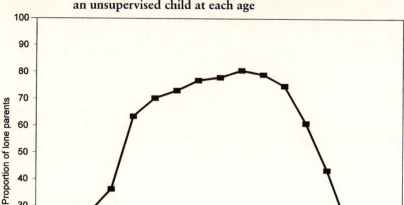

ages for which childcare is both acceptable and in demand as 5-13 years. Two-thirds or more of out-of-work lone parents feel they would need some form of (non-sibling) supervision for a child between these ages if they were to start work of 16 hours or more each week.

As nearly half the lone parents not working 16 hours or more have at least one child aged under five, these findings suggest one reason why the cost or availability of childcare is not (yet) the issue. More than half think their child is too young for childcare. Among out-of-work lone parents as a whole then, a quarter of those who are prepared to consider using childcare think their child too young at the moment.

It is possible to infer from Figure 6.3 that more than two-thirds of parents with an 11 or 12 year-old child would need to use childcare or some form of adult supervision they found acceptable, as would six in ten with a 13 year-old, four in ten with a 14 year-old, and a fifth whose child was 15 years. The 11 year age restriction on the childcare disregard would leave all these parents meeting the full costs of such childcare.

Once again, the youngest ages at which parents felt comfortable using their preferred form of care depended on what that source of care was. Siblings were generally only acceptable once a youngest child was five years or older, but the majority who preferred ex-partners, parents, other relatives or friends, collective provision (nursery schools, crèches) and live-in nannies were happy using them for pre-school children. Among those out-of-work parents choosing the most popular form of care – a registered childminder – equal proportions were happy for the minder to start before the child's fifth birthday as felt the child would need to have reached school-age first.

The National Survey asked parents about arrangements to leave the child unsupervised with which the parent felt *comfortable*. The depth study revealed that working parents undertook 'latchkey' arrangements with which they did not feel comfortable.

> *She's in for 3.40, and I have to trust her with the key. Which is wrong, really, for a 10 year-old: she shouldn't be under that responsibility. I get in at just after four. But coming down that road is so nerve-wracking. I know she wouldn't do anything. But I just think … Like, a few weeks ago, I came in, and she wasn't here. So I phoned my best friend straight away. She says, I'm really sorry, she wanted to come here. But that just caused so much anxiety. And that was frightening.* [Carrie]

Cynth admitted leaving her 10 and 7 year-old children on their own while she worked, to give her teenage daughter time off from caring for her siblings in the evenings.

> *They know not to answer the door. They won't answer the phone. They just let the answerphone go and if they recognise the voice then they'll pick it up. So I mean they just sit and watch the telly. I thought if it had been sort of ten, eleven o'clock I wouldn't have done it but for an hour and an half … it gets [eldest daughter] off my back, she gets her night out.*

As children grew older, and sought to demonstrate their own independence, parents found it more difficult to impose childcare on them. Sharon spoke of this problem arising particularly once her son had moved on to secondary education.

> *You literally will them to grow up faster so that you don't have that torment ... It seems ludicrous that I then say 'Okay you're responsible enough to walk there and back on your own but you're not responsible to stay here half an hour on your own'. That's crazy. I've got to give way sooner or later.*

For Joanna, the need for some form of care for her teenage son was as much an issue of fulfilling her own responsibilities as a mother, as she saw them, than her son's reluctance to use care.

> *They've brought this new thing out about the childminding, where I would get an allowance for [my son]. But what happens to my older boy? 'Cos I'm not the type of mum to just let him come home from school, let himself in, feed himself, I just couldn't ... I know some people say 'But he's 15!' But to me because he's only got – I class myself as mum and dad – one parent, I just feel he's going to walk in and there's nobody.*

Where parents thought childcare necessary for older children, the issue became one of availability. Older children were likely to need only a few hours supervision each week either side of their school hours, a period which childminders were unlikely to consider worthwhile. Few knew of suitable after-school schemes.

> *Childminders won't have 12 year-olds and they don't want one-off. Childminders want regular hours.* [Sian]

So Sian left her son alone at home.

> *I have great feelings of unease about that.*

Conversely, parents who were apprehensive of letting 'strangers' into their homes, or using formal care (Chapter 5), felt better able to justify leaving their children alone in the absence of suitable care. Marion had two children, a 13 and a 14 year-old, the older of whom had a bone disorder.

> *I feel more at home knowing that they're on their own really, than leaving them with someone that I don't know.*

The problem for Jackie whose 15 year-old son was partially deaf, and had related behavioural problems, was getting him to go to school.

> *I know jolly well if I went to work before he went to school, I don't think he'd go to school. I'd have to have someone here in the mornings to make sure he was up for school. But then after school he'd be quite capable. He'd be able to look after himself then.*

Jackie could envisage using her neighbour for this purpose, but would feel obliged to pay for this 'care'.

> *I probably wouldn't have to pay her, but I would out of politeness.*

The question of when children are able to look after themselves while their mothers' work generated answers of the same order as the National Survey, typically 13 or 14 years. Lower ages were nearly always given in the context of care being available from older siblings. Although there is no exact age limit in law, parents commonly thought 14 years a legal minimum.

> *Thirteen, it depends how they grew up. Once they got to 13, I probably still won't trust 'em, 'cos they'd probably start fighting all the time.* [Melanie]

> *Isn't it illegal, anyway? I would have said ... about 14.* [May]

> *My big one is only going to be 13 in May, so I don't think it's good, legally I don't think I could leave the other kids with him, even though he's a responsible child.* [Julie]

Just over half the lone parents not working 16 hours or more are prepared to use childcare and would need to use it: it is for these parents that childcare availability is an issue. It will become an issue for the majority of the remainder – parents who consider their children too young for care – as their children grow up. The first part of this chapter has shown that childcare is still an issue for children in their early teens. Most of the remainder of this chapter assesses parents' knowledge of childcare availability across the age range. It is first worth pausing briefly to consider the other ways in which childcare is needed by a lone parent seeking to take up work.

OTHER NEEDS FOR CHILDCARE

The availability of regular, reliable and suitable childcare is essential if a lone mother is to take up work outside school hours. However, if she is to get a job she considers worthwhile, she will also need childcare to cover her trips to and from job interviews. This care is likely to be one-off and will need to be arranged at short notice on limited resources. The question of temporary childcare was asked of lone parents.

> *What do you do with your children when you go for interview? I had to work interviews round it. I've had to make out that I've not been very well: 'Can I reschedule?' I know that [my ex]'s off, and he can look after [my daughter]. They were ringing me up 'Can you come in this afternoon?' You don't get the job anyway, but you know there's a chance you could get that job.* [Steph]

Parents might also need childcare for job-related training. Rebecca wanted to do a training course which runs from 1pm to 8pm.

> *I want to go back to college in September to finish off me hairdressing, see how that goes, but childminders and money stop me from doing that 'cos it's not school hours.*

Most parents pieced together childcare for interviews on an ad hoc basis. The temporary nature of the demand made parents able to take advantage of friends of relatives they felt unable to call on for longer periods. The problems of childcare availability for training persist. A number of training centres provide free crèches, but parents cannot always afford the course fees.

AVAILABILITY OF CHILDCARE

It was stated in Chapter 1 that the cost and availability of childcare are closely related. Where a free market exists in childcare, finding childcare should only be limited by parents' ability to pay for it. If the potential of each parent to generate the resources to pay for care is taken into account, then more specialist forms of childcare can be seen to be unaffordable. Parents will dismiss, or ignore, sources of care for which their likelihood of gaining access is almost nil. Discussions will focus not on cost but on how to afford the sources of care which the parent can envisage using. If no such sources exist then parents will discuss childcare availability rather than their inability to pay for expensive childcare which is out of their reach.

In seeking to take up work, parents need to find childcare which is affordable given the likely returns they foresee from their employment. Jobs which offer a financial incentive may well have hours which overlap with the school day. Emma, out of work for 16 years, sums up the lack of incentive to work in the absence of suitable childcare.

> *I don't have anybody who would watch the kids for me so that I could work. There's just nobody at all. What kind of job could I get that would allow me to come off Income Support?*

The availability of any expensive formal after-school childcare in her area is irrelevant to her case. It is the absence of low-cost or free childcare outside of school hours which decreases Emma's incentive to work. Her long absence from the labour market suggests she considers part-time work during school hours too poorly paid.

> *There's not a lot of childcare, unless you really know someone that would take your child on and look after them while you went to work. There's nothing around here at all, not full-time as far as I know.* [Jackie]

It was rare for parents to attribute their absence from work solely to availability of care. For most, the education system offered supervision for at least part of the day which would allow parents to consider some part-time work. The availability constraint is then finding care that complements school hours and holidays, or hours of work which fit the time parents foresee as potentially supervised.

> *Maybe nine till three, half past nine till three. Something that would fit in with the kids' hours. But then you've got the problem of the school holidays. I mean, that's always a problem.* [May]

But to hear of job vacancies which fit in with school hours was rare. Ruth intimated that among some employers, such hours were a 'perk', earned after a period of continuous service.

> *A couple of the girls around here work at Sainsbury's during the day and they leave at half past eight in the morning. The kids can go to school at that time and they come back about that time. I think you've to wait three years to get those hours. You have to be there a couple of years before you get the school hours, because they're always so popular.* [Ruth]

> *When they come up, they're snapped up, and the thing is not all of them advertise. A lot of it is word of mouth. It's all friends. They say we're looking for somebody. These are the hours. So they get in first. They don't even get into the paper.* [Cynth]

Ellie, a lone mother of five children of 15 years and younger, was just starting a new job in residential social work, after her long period out of work which included a foundation course in social work. She was adamant that she would prioritise any job which offered school hours over her new career.

> *If it meant starting a job at nine o'clock in the morning and finishing at four o'clock then I'd go for it, I'd go for it, even if it meant changing the course of my career I'd do that.*

Given that childcare has to be arranged, often in quite complicated combinations, and paid for, it is not surprising that parents would prefer jobs which fit within school hours. A clearer indication of the priority lone mothers set on work is their willingness to look beyond the ten to three job when there are few such vacancies in their area.

> *The jobs that I looked at, in the paper, for part-time, said hours were flexible. But they always seemed to overlap. Either they were too early, and finished early, or okay in the afternoon and finished too late. There was never anything set. So, I thought 'Well just go for it'. I remembered I really wanted to go full-time in the first place.* [Steph]

Relying on school for supervised care was not without its draw-backs. Besides holidays and in service days, children will be encouraged to stay away when sick. Parents without a regular source of care would be faced with the stark choice of sending the child to school ill, or taking time off work.

> *I've sent [my daughter] to school ill loads of times, I'll be honest, like coughs, colds. Where, really, she could have done with staying in bed. But I've done that. More often than not, she's been sent, to school. Purely because of my job.* [Carrie]

Parents frequently had to consider jobs which required irregular hours, shift or evening work. They did so either because their experience and expertise was in fields which required such hours or because of the absence of other vacancies. Their existence and suitability for lone mothers should be expected since lone mothers compete for jobs in a segment of the labour market dominated by working mothers in couples. The latter outnumber working lone mothers by more than five to one. Employers have often tailored posts to suit mothers whose partner can cover non-regular work hours (for example, the 'back shift' during the evenings). Such jobs present a need for childcare which extends into the evenings, sometimes overnight, and which is flexible (Kozak, 1994). Lone mothers felt that childcare which covered irregular hours was rare.

> *Nursing's not going to be a possibility for quite a while yet, because it's three shift contracts, and I just couldn't do three shifts. And then I don't know of any childminder that copes with unsocial hours ... even just slightly out the norm and the whole thing would fall apart.* [Maureen]

> *When I was working part-time on nights I couldn't actually get a childminder on a night. They're all sort of basic either full-time or part-time during the day. None actually work on the nights.* [Elaine]

> *The ones I know don't have them after six and they don't have them weekends.* [Cynth]

Others in work had solved such problems with difficulty. Cathy felt her position in work precarious because she relied solely on one babysitter, without whom:

> *...it would be like a different babysitter every day ... a lot of shifting about. It wouldn't be steady for them.* [Cathy]

> *If I knew I was working eleven till four every day, then maybe I'd consider someone picking her up from school but it's not that kind of job. Every week, I get my rota. It looks that way and then you'll get a phone-call, like at nine o'clock Saturday morning. By the way, today you can't finish at four now. It's got to be five. But it's so last-minute. Everything's last-minute. There is no way, if it weren't for mum, that I could have a job like that.* [Carrie]

For parents with young children, the 'free' supervision offered by the education system had yet to become available. Some found low-cost pre-school childcare provision fell short of even 'normal' working hours.

> *What extra would it take to staff a nursery till five? I would say you've got the private nurseries to one extreme – £90 a week which is lot of money unless you've both got really good jobs – and then you go down to maybe about £1 a week. Why couldn't they have something even in between that – maybe people on their own or even couples would be quite happy to pay even £20-25 a week and have them staffed a bit longer.* [Sadie]

Some parents had never looked for childcare and were ignorant of its sources. There might be a problem with childcare availability in their area, but this was not what was stopping them looking for work. Maggie talked a lot about high childcare costs for her three children, but added:

> *I've never put myself into a position where there's been a job where if I can sort the kids out then I can take the job. I haven't looked into it. I don't know about childminders well enough ... I would like to be able to be the one that takes them to school and collects them from school.*

For reasons outlined in the previous chapter, availability was irrelevant for mothers unwilling to consider time apart from their children outside school hours. These lone mothers did not want to share the childcare task. They would consider themselves falling short on the child-rearing role they saw as their main priority at present.

> *I wouldn't consider for example a job from before nine o'clock. I feel that's my responsibility to take her to school and to take her out when I can. That's what I would like to do as well.* [Judith]

Only part-time work allows parents to fulfil both their child-rearing and work objectives. Sandra was able to do so, working 25 hours each week, with help from her parents taking her son to school.

> *I don't know if I would go the whole day 'cos I don't think it's really fair to him, because he wouldn't see me in the morning then it'd be after teatime before he would see me again, and then it's not long till he's in his bed. The only time would be the weekend and that's really not fair.*

But part-time work may carry other disadvantages besides poor financial return. Following her recent job termination, Jenny associated part-time work with poor job security.

> *The jobs I've looked at, they're temporary and I don't want a temporary job. With a full-time job you've got your money coming in. It's not going to stop just like that, like this one did.*

Another means by which parents might circumvent the issue of childcare availability would be to work at home. Aside from a tiny minority with the resources to set up their own business, outworking provided the main source of this type of work. It could be argued that outworking, or home working, would represent an ideal means for lone parents to return to the labour market. But only 3 per cent of lone parents in employment work solely from home, and a small proportion of these will be self-employed businesswomen. The study collected little evidence for why home working was unpopular. Only one depth interview respondent spoke of her experience of home working. Despite repeated attempts, she found the financial return from such work offered little incentive to continue.

> *That was from home. But the hours you had to do to make the money, it was too many ... It's like Christmas crackers and things like that, it's a rip-off to be honest with you ... painting soldiers, I've tried that ... Typewriters...*

If it is hard for lone mothers to find and accept jobs which do not present a need for childcare, then finding childcare is a prerequisite for work entry.

AVAILABILITY OF DIFFERENT CHILDCARE SOURCES

Lone parent families need different kinds of childcare which depend on the child's age, hours of work, personal preferences and the perceived financial resources available. Childcare studies categorise care in similar ways: usually in terms of the care environment, collective, shared or one-to-one, legal status and the relationship between the carer and the child (see Meltzer, 1994 for detailed description; Marsh and McKay, 1993a). The categories used in Chapter 2 are typical of these. Parents also tended to discuss childcare in these terms, although they might generalise more broadly to formal and informal provision. There is of course some definitional overlap between sources: when does a babysitter become an unregistered childminder, what if the children's grandmother is already a registered childminder? And the distinction, if any, parents made between state-run educationally-orientated nursery schools and private nurseries or crèches with an educational element might be more in terms of ages, hours and cost than the care environment.

Formal childcare facilities provided free or at nominal cost for pre-school children were commonly reported as available locally. Most often state nursery schools fulfilled this function, although the hours rarely matched most job vacancies. Children might be restricted to morning or afternoon sessions only, perhaps only two hours long each day, or to certain days of the week. The school would cover one or, at most, two years in advance of the child's progression to statutory schooling. A further problem was posed by the administration of school waiting lists which favoured those who did not move house. Lone parents whose children were born within a partnership might be disadvantaged in two ways since the need for such childcare might arise only once the partnership split up. First, if they did not anticipate the need to register in time, they might miss out on nursery school provision. Second, such parents also frequently change residence as a result of their partnership breakdown or of the council housing policy, and might be registered in the wrong area. The limited number of places available meant chances of getting a place were diminished.

> *Hit or miss whether they get in or not.* [Cathy]

Playgroups tend to be available for a limited number of hours each week, and then only at a price. The few parents who used them did so for the quality of care, not to cover working hours.

> *I think like professional carers at a playgroup are very good in a way. I think children aren't usually cheeky to people. Like if [my son] went to playgroup he would be as good as gold. He wouldn't say boo to a goose. If they tell him off he'll probably go 'Oh my God' and that would be it, but with a relative he'd probably push them a little bit further.* [Jess]

No depth interview respondents used a private nursery, crèche or a nanny. Childminders were the most commonly used form of formal care provision, and parents' positive and negative impressions of childcare reported in Chapters 5 and 6 were largely focused on the childminders they knew and used or had used. Most minders worked from their own homes. Some preferred younger children whom they cared for throughout the day. Others collected children from the school gates. Still others took children across a wide range of ages. Waiting lists were again common.

Older children might find the type of care offered by a childminder stifling, or dislike the company of younger children also in her care. Parents often reported difficulties finding care suitable for school-age children not yet old enough to stay at home, or even travel home, unsupervised.

> *I feel that they are too old for a childminder.* [Emma]

One solution which has emerged over the past 20 years, and recently boosted through set-up grants from Training and Enterprise Councils (TECs), is out-of-school childcare (Sanderson and Percy-Smith, 1995). Such care takes the form of after-school schemes and school holiday schemes, often based at the school. Evening activities might contain an educational element, such as time to do homework. During holidays, activities – sports, swimming, trips out – might be promoted.

Some parents knew of such schemes, others mistook the out-of-school label to mean youth clubs. Interviewers were briefed to describe the out-of-school childcare concept. For some lone parents, this was the first they had heard.

> *That would be ideal, wouldn't it? That would be perfect.* [May]

Maureen knew of an after-school service which covered holidays and in-service days.

> *My first choice would be after-school and I know there's a waiting list for that, so I would be on the list for that ... [For] the school term. I think it's £42 a week. But they'll pick the kids up which makes a difference, and they'll take them to school in the morning ... I think it's eight till six, so you would just scrape by and no more.*

The extra hour Maureen's scheme covered in the morning would have made all the difference to Sue.

> *She could go in the after-school club in the afternoon, but I still need somebody to take her to school in the morning, so I'd rather go for a childminder, than if I split it. Otherwise I'd have a childminder to take her in the morning and she'd go to the school in the afternoon.*

Two working parents were also critical of holiday schemes in their areas.

> *They're not convenient. They don't start at 7.30 in the morning and they don't go on till 6.30. They don't provide lunches and they're not safe. They're run by student girls who've got no experience ... They are not geared for working parents. They are geared*

*for people who just want to put their children somewhere, the bore-
dom element.* [Shirley]

*That's when kids start mixing with the wrong kids and I don't want
that to start. I don't want to live here for very long ... Anyone
could send their kids there for £6 a week.* [Sasha]

Sasha was reluctant to use a scheme which other parents could
afford. But she was not in a position to pay for care which would
isolate her children from the 'wrong' children. She had already
reported how the cost of childcare encouraged her to reduce her
hours to 'part-time' (22 each week). She had ruled out using any
collective provision that she too could afford. Instead, she used
her mother-in-law (a registered childminder).

Employer provision

No working lone mother reported using childcare facilities at their
place of employment. Just 2 per cent of working lone parents (five
people) in the National Survey said they made use of childcare
facilities provided by their employer. It is thus no surprise that
out-of-work parents viewed the prospects of in-work childcare as
very slim.

*No companies around here have any sort of facilities or ideals for
working mothers. I mean if you want to be a working mother
you've just got to basically forget the children, really.* [Sally]

Availability of informal sources

The benefits and disadvantages of other informal sources, such as
grandparents, aunts and friends, have been discussed in the pre-
ceding chapter. The availability of such sources varied between
parents. A substantial minority of out-of-work parents do not have
such sources available to them. Potential informal carers may also
work or have other caring demands. Family members may live too
far way, be ill or deceased. There may be animosity between the
parent and relatives or friends. The lack of a contractual agree-
ment makes some parents more reluctant to take friends or family
on as carers. It may be even more difficult to assess the returns

from working if the care is (as yet) unpriced. A reciprocal arrangement may need to be negotiated, or financial terms agreed.

Rural areas

Most lone parents live in urban areas. It is fair to assume that within a few miles of each parent's home exist a range of childcare sources, such as childminders, nursery schools and crèches, in addition to any family, friends, babysitters or other informal sources. These sources may be 'unavailable' because they are too expensive, inaccessible, inappropriate or over-subscribed, but they are likely to exist. This is an important point that is difficult to prove, because no national inventory exists of childcare providers.[1]

This existence is not something that can be assumed with any certainty in rural areas. Childcare providers will be more dispersed and there may be certain forms of care for which demand is simply too low to justify provision. This may leave lone mothers in rural areas without suitable childcare provision. Maureen had given up her job because she had been unable to find suitable childcare in a rural community.

> *I think there were five childminders. If you got one to accept you, you were doing awful well. It wasn't that we picked them, they picked us. They could pick and choose and have anybody they wanted. They were guaranteed the money, so it was a case of: your face fitted with them they would take your baby.* [Maureen]

> *I know a woman that's a registered childminder. She's that good, you're speaking maybe about a three or four year waiting list just to get your child in.* [Meg]

Scarcity of childcare in rural areas could also raise prices. Tracy found herself paying out more than she earned as a retainer in order to keep the only childminder in her village.

> *During the summer holidays, it's a nightmare ... I had to ask her, 'Could you not make it a weekly rate rather than an hourly one?' because it was coming to nearly £200 a week just for childcare*

CHILDREN WITH LONG-TERM ILLNESS OR DISABILITIES

Parents have spoken of the difficulties they had finding suitable childcare. These problems are magnified where the child requires specialised care (Philp and Duckworth, 1982). The required forms of care may be more expensive, and the need for care may be prolonged into the child's teenage or early adulthood. Lone parents of children with a long-term illness or disability may find it more difficult to surmount the childcare barrier and return to work. Marie had a son with Down's Syndrome who required additional care.

> *Where you've got three children and one of them is handicapped, it's a lot to ask somebody to look after three children. When you've got one that's more to look after than the other two.*

Care demands also weighed heavily in the thoughts of parents of children whose illnesses presented less predictable demands. Sian felt the anticipated progression of her son's illness would make her position in work more precarious.

> *Adolescence is a difficult time for diabetics. Their metabolism changes so quickly that very often they are unstable and again you are in and out of hospital.*

And other long-term complaints like asthma (common among lone parents' children) could jeopardise employment as much through other people's ignorance as the demands of the disorder itself.

> *She has a fair amount of time off school. Most of her asthma presents as a cough, which is irritating. I can just switch it off, but it's dreadful for the kids at school. And the school is really just not happy to have her. They're just not, because she's coughing all day through the class so I'm inclined just to keep her off. A couple of times they've phoned me and said would I come and pick her up. They panic about the medication 'Well, she's had this amount of inhaler, and could she have any more?'... I'll just come and lift her out and then it's not their problem any more, because they'd be on the phone every two minutes.* [Maureen]

Other parents could identify definite health problems exacerbated by the use of childcare. Frequently these concerned asthmatic or allergic reactions.

> *I used to sometimes leave them with the lady down the road. I would have her kids quite a lot and [my son]'s got asthma and she smokes like a trooper and [my son] would come back coughing and wheezing like anything. Not an ideal situation.* [Ruth]

> *I just don't have anybody else who could look after them. Sometimes they go up for the day to their other grandparents. I can't let them stay up there for too long because [my daughter] gets asthma, and they're got three small fine-haired dogs there, and she comes home with really bad asthma. I used to let them stay overnight, but I don't now.* [Sally]

Ruth was out of work at the time of interview but Sally had been able to leave the children with their other grandmother. Julie's son also had asthma.

> *Sometimes he's not well, let's say for two weeks suddenly, and then sometimes he's well for three months.*

The persistence of complaints and illness of many kinds could inhibit lone parents' ability to commit continuous periods of their day to an employer. In the less severe cases, the use of continuous childcare might seem difficult to justify, and few outside the family would provide the intermittent care needed if the mother's work is to remain uninterrupted. For the more severe cases, occasional or more permanent specialised care might be available, and even free. But rarely are such sources a suitable cover for a working mother, particularly one with no current partner (Beresford, 1995). An assumption is that mothers are permanently on hand to offer unpaid care (Baldwin, 1985). Marie had bad experiences using respite care and was reluctant to do so again.

> *I was getting respite care, for [my son] for one week of every month. It took them a long time to talk me into letting him do this. Eventually, I let him go. He's been there a year. They set a chap on. He'd only been there about three weeks when he sexually abused my lad. He was only a young bloke, he was only in his twenties.*

Because of [my son] being what he is, and there was nobody saw him, he's got away with it. So this man is now still working there, but my son doesn't go there no more. I stopped it. So I don't get any respite care for [my son]. No help whatsoever.

Arrangements for her son's school bus had been changed so it now longer picked him up from his home, but at the end of the road. The need to accompany her son and the unreliability of the bus took even more time from her potential working day.

I have to be up there for five past eight in the morning: the bus is supposed to be there for ten past. It's never there for ten past. And it's supposed to drop him off at the top of the road at twenty past. It's never there for twenty past.

Following the introduction of the walk and wait for the bus, her son had become less willing to attend. His refusal to attend school on some days further reduced Marie's ability to seek work.

EMERGENCY ARRANGEMENTS

Simply finding a source of affordable childcare may not resolve the barriers to work entry lone parents perceive. Whatever childcare arrangements are adopted, there is a risk that on some days they may not be available, or they may break down at short notice. Parents may only feel confident enough about their childcare to start work if some form of back-up has also been arranged. While not being the primary source, such care will need to meet the minimum requirements for quality parents hold. Most often the fallback care was family-based. For Sue it was her father.

There have been a couple of times, where one of my childminders said 'Oh I forgot to tell you, we're going out for the day'. So I just had to rely on my dad then to help me out.

And for Cynth, her daughter had to take time off school to care for her brother. With exams looming for her daughter, however, Cynth was contemplating misleading her employer in order to provide the cover herself at times when her son was ill.

There was no way I could afford to take the time off work, because 1) I lose the money and 2) I'd have to catch up on the hours anyway, so I said to her, 'Can you stay at home and look after him?'. She had to stay at home. It didn't bother her at the time but she's got her exams next year ... I'll just phone in sick myself. That's the only way I can get round it. I say it's me that's ill because that way I still get paid.

Two parents, Janet and Sally, spoke of the reciprocal support they had negotiated from friends when their childcare broke down.

I take two children. My friend at the moment, she works half past eight till one. So I take her children to school. If I leave work, if I've got anything on in the afternoon and can't pick the children up for any reason, she always has them. [Janet]

She fell over and broke her foot. Now this really was a worry 'cos I mean this is a long-term thing. And of course she couldn't do anything, she just had to sit and I thought, 'Well I'm going to have to give up work, because [my employer] just wouldn't accommodate me at all, to taking the kids in the morning and hoping that somebody else would take them home'. Then eventually we just worked it out. Other mothers said 'We'll take them home and you pick up them, or we'll take them to your mother's or we'll pick them if you drop them off to our house in the morning, we'll take them'. [Sally]

Thus childcare might break down because the childminder becomes ill herself.

Cynth expressed reluctance to use the reciprocal arrangements she had.

One's a couple of doors away and the other one's at the top of the road. If I really get stuck, Brenda and Paul. The thing is Paul has done it but it's not when I've gone to work ... But I'd rather do it off my own back, 'cos at the end of the day I can say 'Well I did it myself'. I've got nobody to answer to.

Cynth and Sally's accounts are borne out by other anecdotal evidence of strong support networks among lone mothers. Nonetheless, some felt too intimidated by their immediate social environment to seek to establish such networks. Michelle, 40, lived apart from her boyfriend, geographically and financially, while he studied at university. She lived with her seven year-old son in a rough neighbourhood:

> *I don't know anybody who is a single parent, not around here any-way. Mind you, I don't speak to anybody. It's too scary.*

There is a very diverse pool of potential childcare to which parents have differential access. The range is restricted first by parents' knowledge of what is available, and second by parents' own preferences and views on what constitutes acceptable care. The third barrier is matching known available suitable childcare to the vacancies available and deciding the financial viability of such a combination. Finally, the arrangement may only be tenable when suitable back-up care has also been arranged.

LONE PARENTS AND THE CHILDCARE BARRIER

The report has established a range of reasons why childcare may or may not pose a barrier to employment for lone mothers. The orientations of mothers towards work, home and family have been examined in Chapter 3 to set the context in which relevance of the cost and availability of childcare can be determined. Chapter 4 carefully drew out parents' perceptions of the financial incentive work offered, including the role played by childcare cost. Chapter 5 looked further at why parents think certain types of childcare suitable or unsuitable, and the effect of their preferences, and those of their children, on the range of care they would be prepared to use. This chapter assessed the extent of families' need for childcare: how, when and where different forms of care are available.

Readers should by now feel familiar with the rationale underlying at least a number of lone mothers' intentions to work or stay at home, and the practical problems they face trying to realise those intentions.

The study has set out to identify those for whom the cost and availability of childcare are the major constraints on entering and staying in work, those for whom it is only one of many concerns, and those lone mothers for whom the childcare issue is largely

Table 1.1 Respondent pseudonyms and group membership codes

	A Affordability of childcare is the issue	B In-work costs of childcare is the issue	C Availability of childcare is the issue	D Neither availa- bility nor cost of childcare is the issue
Employment status at time of interview				
In work 16+ hours each week	Tanya Tracy	Alison	Carrie** Cathy Claire Cynth*	Steph Sasha Shirley* Samantha** Sue Sonia** Sian** Sharon Sophie* Sarah Susan Sandra Sadie Sally*
Not in work 16+ hours each week	Maureen** Maxine May Maggie** Maria Michelle Marsha* Meg Melanie** Mary Margaret Marion* Marie**	Rebecca Ruth* Rachel	Elaine Esther Elizabeth Ellie Eileen Emma	June Janice Jane Jill Jackie* Jess Josie Julie** Janine** Judith Joanna Jenny* Janet Jean**

* denotes parents of a child with long-term or limiting illness or disability,
** denotes children where these require additional care

irrelevant. The answer to the study question comes from explaining membership of each group (Table 1.1). For simplicity, the characteristics of the four groups of lone mothers outlined in Chapter 1 are repeated.

A: Those for whom the affordability of childcare is the major barrier to entering or staying in work (including one for whom cost would be an issue were it not for her agoraphobia, and one other who simply cannot contemplate paying for care and is consequently not seeking work) (15 mothers).

Only two of this group, Tracy and Tanya, had overcome the childcare barrier and work 16 hours or more each week. They still felt constrained by the cost of childcare. Tanya felt she had run up against the (unspoken) limit on hours of childcare her mother could offer, and could not afford the leap to nanny fees for the evening work that would accompany planned restructuring of her hours at work. Childcare costs mean Tracy's net income is negative during the summer holidays.

The remainder had no paid work and represented a third of those out of work. These were people who intended to work and whose arguments for not working centred on the lack of a financial incentive due to the need to pay for childcare. Most were actually seeking work. The exceptions were Mary, Meg and Marie. Mary's agoraphobia prevented her seeking work. Marie did not because her son has Down's Syndrome: she would do so if she could afford to pay someone to look after him. Meg had not been able to take up work because her free source of childcare, her mother, had moved.

B: Those who identify childcare as part of a group of in-work costs (housing costs, travel, clothing) which reduce their incentive to work (four mothers).

Alison was the sole worker in this category. She felt that the financial returns from work (including Family Credit) minus her in-work costs were less than she would receive on Income Support. This was eroding her motivation to stay in work. The others attributed the problems they faced taking up work to a set of in-work costs of which childcare was one. For Ruth, these costs included mortgage interest payments. Rebecca, who was seeking work at the time of interview, was concerned about increased rent, council tax and school meal payments.

C: Those who identify the availability of suitable care as the problem, but not its cost (10 mothers).

For two mothers, Ellie and Emma, it was their large family sizes and older children which posed problems locating childcare. For

others, Esther, Elaine, Eileen, Carrie and Claire, it was the restricted range of childcare sources they were prepared to consider.
Elaine, for example, would use her parents only for short periods,
and distrusted 'strangers'. Yet others, Elizabeth, Cathy and Cynth,
could find work only at hours for which suitable childcare was not
available. Both Cathy and Cynth had entered work in the three
months prior to interview

*D: Those for whom childcare cost/availability is not a problem
(this is a broad group ranging from those who do not want or
expect to be able to work and those who doubt that they could
earn enough to make a job worth doing, irrespective of the issue of
childcare, to those who earn so much that childcare cost is immaterial). This group includes people who have problems with childcare,
but crucially no one who is stopped from working by its cost or
availability (28 mothers).*

These were half those interviewed. Four, Janine, Janet, Joanna and
June, were simply averse to being apart from their children. Nine
others were similarly not motivated to do (more) work even
though cheap or free childcare was available. One mother, Julie,
found it difficult to envisage the work she could get covering the
costs of her large family. For Janice legal problems over her residential status and racial discrimination were more important
factors than the cost of childcare. The workers included seven professional women who had nearly always worked and could not
envisage their lives without work. Some in this position, like Sadie,
Sonia, Samantha and Steph, found their financial position worsen-
ing through low pay and in-work costs. Sadie, Sonia and Samantha
had free childcare. Sadie's and Samantha's positions were likely to
improve once their Family Credit claims had been processed.
Sasha and Sandra – less skilled – had low-cost childcare provided
by parents without whom they could not maintain their mid-range
hours (22-25 hours a week). Sarah combined earnings and maintenance to lift her income above Income Support levels. She felt able
to pay for a childminder either side of school hours.

So, for a third of parents (those in Groups A and B), childcare
cost was at least part of the problem in taking up work. There
were some contrasts between the mothers in these two groups and
those others for whom cost was not the issue. Mothers receiving
maintenance were over-represented in group D (10 of the 15 who

received maintenance from a former partner). Only one mother in Group A and one in Group B received maintenance.

Group D contained disproportionate shares of the better-qualified, of home owners and of those who lived in their parent's houses. Interestingly, those with qualifications above 'O' level in Group D were equally divided between the in- and out-of-work.

Young parents were more likely to be found in Group A: half aged under 25 years have childcare costs as the major problem. While this may be related to the presence of very young children, there were few differences in the role of childcare between parents whose youngest was pre-school age and those whose youngest was aged five to ten. Within Group D, however, children's age did make a difference: those with a youngest child aged five to ten were more than twice as likely to be in work of 16+ hours than those with a youngest aged under four years. All but one parent whose youngest was aged 11 years or more was in group D. Thus even where childcare costs may not be the issue, young children constrain some mothers from entering the labour market for other reasons, such as the mothers' reluctance to spend time apart from their children.

These divisions are characteristic of those which earlier studies have associated with lone parents' level of attachment to the labour market (dubbed the 'benefit fault line' by Marsh, 1994). Work is more attractive to parents who stand to lose less of each pound in work because they do not pay rent and have some exempt non-work income from maintenance. It is interesting that the same partition applies here in identifying the role played by the cost of childcare, not simply attachment to work.

One 'benefit fault line' division does not apply. There is no association between the former marital status of the parent and the role of childcare. Parents who never lived with a partner are as likely to see and experience childcare costs as a barrier to work as are divorcees. And contrary to an earlier hypothesis, never-partnered parents are if anything less likely to have problems with the *availability* of childcare than are parents separated from marriage, but the differences are small.

What was the outcome for families? One outcome measure used in successive PRILIF surveys is a measure of relative material hardship.[2] A quarter of depth interview respondents – all but one of them out of work – had been found in severe hardship at the time of the National Survey. There was a strong association between the role of childcare and hardship. Half those in severe hardship said childcare costs were the main reason keeping them out of work. Indirectly, therefore, the cost of childcare was the main reason why half of our respondents who experienced severe hardship were in this state.

So lone mothers for whom childcare cost was the primary consideration were typically younger, less well qualified, less likely to be in receipt of maintenance and more likely to be tenants than other lone mothers.

Notes

1 The largest childcare database in the UK is that managed privately by Childcare Solutions, which includes details of nanny agencies, holiday play schemes, nurseries, out-of-school clubs and Local Authority registered childminders. Nonetheless, informal sources, such as non-agency babysitters, relatives and friends, are beyond its remit.

2 A 7-point index (lowest=0, highest=6) of relative financial and material hardship was constructed, adding one point for each 'yes' answer to the following questions:

Does the family have:

1 Two or more problem debts?
2 Two or more items on the food list scored 'unable to afford'?
3 Three or more items on the clothing and leisure lists scored 'unable to afford'?
4 Four or more items on the consumer durables list scored 'unable to afford'?
5 Both the financial anxiety measures scored at the highest point ('Always worried about money' and 'In deep financial trouble')?
6 Both the questions asking for spontaneous estimates of items needed for adults and children named by respondent?

A further threshold, scoring three or more points, was used to distinguish families in severe hardship.

Chapter 7

RECONCILING THE LABOUR AND CHILDCARE MARKETS

The earlier chapters demonstrated that lone mothers weighing up the decision to enter work and use childcare try to reconcile two otherwise independent markets – of job vacancies and of childcare – with the needs of themselves *and their children*. Women with often distant memories of work and no direct experience of childcare find this a difficult alignment to get into focus and balance. The job must offer hours for which childcare can be found, and offer a net profit which is worthwhile. This profit has to be worked out by comparing earnings from work with its costs; in-work versus out-of-work benefit entitlements; the cost of matching and paying for suitable childcare; any incidental costs associated with low-cost provision (such as the opportunity and cash cost of caring for a friend's children) and other in-work costs. The parent must decide whether the final income compensates sufficiently for her own time and effort, separation from her children and the effect on the children themselves. The lone parent needs to find both a job and childcare which together produce this positive outcome.

Strictly speaking, childcare can be said to be affordable, or not affordable, only in the context of a specific job opportunity. Parents will need to know about one if they are to evaluate the other. But both childcare and work are supplied by imperfect markets, about which the lone mother will have imperfect knowledge. The level of in-work benefit depends on both the job and the childcare, such that the lone mother is also unlikely to be fully aware of her benefit entitlement should she take up work. Parents with a limited knowledge of available childcare or the benefit system will find it difficult to do full justice in considering a job vacancy. Some may err on the side of caution and remain on Income Support, others may be over-optimistic and find their in-work income package falls short of their expectations. Still others may experiment with a new job, being prepared to leave it if it doesn't work out.

Given that vacancies will offer wage rates within known limits, and that only a subset of vacancies will be open to the lone parent, she can be fairly certain that childcare above a certain price is nearly always out of her reach. Likewise the ability to use cheaper or more preferred sources of childcare during certain hours of the day will influence the types of job vacancy considered. The role played by childcare in the decision to work is closely related to which one lone parents prioritise – the job or the childcare – and what, if any, effect this has on their success in taking up work. This chapter is concerned with this process of matching up the suitable childcare available locally with appropriate job vacancies.

Preparing the Ground

Lone parents were encouraged to elaborate on how they would go about arranging childcare should a suitable vacancy arise. For many respondents out of work the suitable vacancy discussed was the scenario Job B (see Chapter 4). Later on, a more general discussion focused on the ease with which vacancies and childcare could be matched locally. Topic guides were constructed in this way on the assumption that in the decision to take up work, it was the job search which came first, and that childcare would be chosen in the context of each job opportunity.

It became clear that for a substantial minority, the assumption that the job came first did not hold. Parents saw a limited range of available and suitable care and prioritised their children's needs to the extent that they considered only the kinds of job that matched a fixed childcare arrangement.

> *Childcare comes first. You've got to make sure you have the childcare 'cos you can't go for the job if you've not got the childcare.*
> [Jenny]

Rebecca and Steph had prearranged their childcare.

I actually went and saw her prior to sort of looking for work, I said to her 'In the event of me finding a job…' [Rebecca]

I'd got her lined up. [Steph]

In this way the parents' existing knowledge of childcare sources, and their personal preferences for care would constrain the range of jobs the parent would consider.

Of course, some parents for whom the prospect of taking up work was more distant might not have any childcare arrangement in mind. But the principle that childcare came first could still apply, as evidenced by these parents' intentions to trial run childcare before taking up work.

I'd have to meet them and the kids would have to meet them beforehand, because if the kids said 'Oh no', then no, because I trust their instincts. [Cynth]

I suppose I'd leave them for a few hours, for a few days, to see how she was with them. [Maxine]

Carrie had already decided that her mother was to provide the childcare should she find the job, but she recognised how this restricted her choices.

I've got to find a job where: I like it: it's got to be able to suit me, suit [my daughter], and suit mum. It's got to suit three people, not just one. That's really hard to do.

Most other parents seeking work and who had not yet designated their preferred sources, would leave the decision until after the job offer had materialised. Maria put this down to her pessimism about getting a job. She was evidently less gloomy about the prospects of finding childcare.

If I get a job then I'll worry about a childminder, instead of the other way around. I'm not looking into all this 'cos I don't think that I'm going to get a suitable job. I think, if one does come along, then I'll start worrying about a childminder.

Meg was also less concerned about finding suitable childcare.

> *I would get the cheapest one first, see how that goes ... A lot of childminders don't take on till nine o'clock and if you've got a job that starts at 7.30...*

Jane lacked self-confidence and felt very isolated socially. She spoke explicitly of the dilemma of reconciling childcare demands with a job vacancy. She had not yet decided which search to begin first.

> *The only thing I think about now is do I find a job first and then get childcare, or do I get that sorted out and then hope that I can get a job. I'm not quite sure how it works. If they want a next week start, where do I go from there?*

Parents intending to work divided on whether childcare or the job vacancy came first. One contributor to the division was the degree of confidence parents had in locating either. Another factor was the relative importance parents placed on their different roles: child-rearing or working. It was the aspect upon which most restrictions were placed which was arranged first. Parents who would only consider a certain type of childcare would seek work with this source in mind. Parents who felt restricted in the types of work they could do, or were likely to be offered, prioritised the job search.

Other influences: childcare discrimination

Other factors acted to complicate decisions about work and childcare. A number of parents spoke of occasions on which they had experienced discrimination from employers because they were lone mothers. In such a situation there was no straight sequence of arranging childcare and work, since employers might prejudge the childcare situation in their decision to offer the job. With or without prearranged childcare, suitable vacancies might not materialise.

> *You go for an interview and I'm asked what age my children are, which I believe they're not allowed to do because they wouldn't ask a man that, and what childcare facilities, and what I would do if*

they were ill ... They actually told me 'We've given it to somebody whose children are teenagers. We know you can do the job, but we felt we couldn't give it to you because you're slightly younger, you've got young children and you might get pregnant again' ... The form I filled in just now for this place asks you what age your children are. [Tracy]

It is possible that media stereotyping of lone parent families influenced this decision by Tracy's potential employer. Such explicit discrimination left Tracy understandably indignant, while others, like Marie, had almost resigned themselves to employers' focus on her childcare arrangements.

I've been for jobs, and I've had good qualifications for the jobs that I've been for. But the unfortunate thing is, they'll say to you, 'Well, have you got somebody that can look after the kids?' 'Yes', and 'What about the school holidays? These people are not going to have your children all day' ... You can't blame them for not wanting you when you've got school holidays and things like that. [Marie]

Because [my son] was so young she did say to me when I was interviewed about him: I wouldn't be taking time off and things like that, because I couldn't get anybody to watch him. [Sandra]

Discrimination of this type on the part of employers puts yet more jobs out of the reach of lone parents, restricting their choices further. It may also confuse their priorities. Discrimination may make arranging childcare relatively easier than finding work, but nonetheless a prerequisite.

Discrimination could take other forms. Maxine felt her employer acted unreasonably when she stated her intention to supplement her wages with Family Credit to meet her childcare costs.

I went for a job as a care assistant. I told her I had children: she says 'All right'. I says, 'I have got a child-minder'. 'Cos I had one fixed up. And she goes, 'Well, how would you manage on the money?' I says, 'I'll claim Family Credit'. And she wouldn't have none of it: she went 'No, forget it'. She told me to leave, because I said I'd claim Family Credit. [Maxine]

If employers become known for discriminating against lone mothers, it may further discourage the search for work. Alternatively parents may seek out employers whose practices are more enlightened.

> *I just phoned up [the employer] ... she gives single parents a better chance ... because a lot of employers round here wouldn't take on single parents.* [Meg]

Once in work, employers' attitudes could still reduce the attractiveness of employment. Sian, a skilled professional, had changed jobs several times to ensure her line manager had a flexible attitude towards her child-rearing responsibilities.

> *I've moved jobs in order to get away from somebody whose attitude was not compatible ... It was the biggest reason for the last move because I was working for somebody who was not flexible and showed no understanding of the fact that you had any other commitments at all.*

Others who might not have the luxury of switching jobs so readily also found that employers' attitudes made a major difference to their ability to take up work. Rebecca worked in a sub-post office before its closure forced her out of work.

> *I used to put him on the bus actually there by the post office. He'd come off the bus. He'd walk into the shop. They'd give him something out of the freezer or something in the microwave. He'd sit and watch telly in the back room and I'd be there until half past four or whatever and it was ideal.*

Lone parents also complained of a shortage of local vacancies, a high level of competition for jobs and age discrimination. These problems are not specific to lone mothers and can affect all job-seekers, but may weigh more heavily for lone parents facing discrimination, inflexible employers or problems arranging and paying for childcare. Without reliable childcare, lone mothers are immediately disadvantaged in any competition for a job vacancy with someone who does not care for children. Failure to secure work could leave parents out of the labour market, with inadequate work experience. The problems of entering the labour market when children were older, after a lengthy break, were explained by Marie.

> *Your children are young, and your family – who can look after them – their children are young. So they can't look after them, they've got enough to look after they own. And you get older as your children get older and theirs have got older. And they've got more time for you. You're too old to get a job, because nobody wants you. 'Cos you've aged! It is a catch-22.*

Any break in contact with the labour market could damage job prospects. So finding a match between the childcare and labour markets could prove essential for a lone parent intending to work at any stage, and the match was needed sooner rather than later.

Parents seeking work adopted a strategy which centred on risk management. Whichever of work or childcare was subject to the greater constraint was arranged first. If the parent placed a range of restrictions on the types of childcare that could be used, then a job opportunity was sought which fitted the parameters of available, suitable childcare. If the type of work that could be undertaken was more restricted or vacancies were few, then childcare became the secondary consideration. Thus the risk of not being able to take up work was minimised.

'QUALITY' TIME

A process by which the childcare and labour markets could be reconciled has been identified. But how did parents decide whether a particular combination of job and childcare would succeed? What gains were needed from a childcare-plus-work package which would outweigh the losses due to separation of parent and child and reduced time at home? Could the equation be balanced solely in financial terms?

The gain appeared to be measured in terms of changes in the quality of the time parents and children spent together. If families were left with some time together, time which carried a higher value because of the parent's paid work, then smaller amounts of time judged better quality could outweigh the loss of longer but less rewarding periods spent together. Any financial gains from employment could be devoted to the time spent together: children might benefit materially or from more visits or trips out.

> *I just want more money basically. It sounds like that's all my concerns. My first concern is my children, giving them some sort of quality of life.* [Maggie]

> *I'd like the job for the money, so I can give them the things what they can't have now.* [Maxine]

The value of time together could also be enhanced by the effect of employment on the parent's mood or orientation to her children in the remaining time she had with them.

> *If you're actually at work you actually give the kids more quality time. It's too easy when you're with them all the time to just sit with them and talk with them, but you don't really do as much. When I'm at work, we still do go places now. But it gives you an incentive to take them somewhere or do more things with them.* [Elaine]

> *The worst thing is to bring children up in an unhappy atmosphere and I think that some people are unhappy not working. It's to do with children and security.* [Sian]

> *If we were going to be better off financially, then I don't really regard it would be that big a sacrifice for her ... so she would have to put up with this, but she would get rewards for it, and I think she'd also have a saner mother ... I don't think the time really matters, I think it's what we're going to do with the time that's important.* [Maureen]

The issue was clearly one of balance, and structural factors might intervene to reduce one or other necessary component: insufficient work, poor wages or too few remaining hours together. Cathy spoke as one for whom the balance had swung too far towards the material benefits of working, at the expense of the family's time together.

I'd like to have more time with them. I think they would like more time as well, but they like all the luxuries that they get along with my working.

And for Emma who was out of work.

I'm here with them all the time but I'm not doing things with them. I probably would speak to them a wee bit more even if I was out working. But the way he is, I just feel like 'Go out of my way!'.

And some very specific times were important to lone parents, such as collecting the children at the end of the school day.

The only thing that I could see that would stop me working would be if it was directly affecting [my daughter] emotionally. I mean she's had me at home now and in the quality time which is like from 4.30 to 8, I've always been here, I've always picked her up, if she's got problems at school then they're dealt with at 3.30 at the gate, I'll go back into class to find out what's happening. [Esther]

It's alright having all the money in the world but you've got to spend some time with your kids as well. It's no good having everything in the house and giving them everything they want but not spending any time with them. [Rebecca]

Some parents felt the balance could not be achieved in their circumstances. The moving targets of childcare needs and costs would never balance with the hours and wages they anticipated from employment.

It will be at least 10 or 11 years before my youngest isn't of school age and that depends upon what they want to do in future life and if they want to carry on with education or not. But I can't actually see a life for me working and being self sufficient until the children are no longer my responsibility ... when they start earning money, then I can. [Maggie]

Parents bore sole responsibility for the decision to enter work. If separation could not be justified in financial and social terms, parents would feel guilty. Meg had stopped working recently.

I felt right guilty because I wasn't there and I was her mum.

In some cases parents were quite specific about seeking a reward for amount of time apart from family: an incentive to part from their children.

I've got his name down for a nursery. I should imagine that would be a half day. I don't know if I could leave him all day. I don't ... perhaps if the work was the incentive then I'd have to. But I think he's a bit young. [Jane]

I'd be thinking about her. But also, I'd be thinking about the wage-packet at the end of the week. [Rachel]

Thus parents could physically arrange their return to work, and justify a new mix of increased income and reduced family time together. Parents could also find employment improved the variety and quality of their own lives. Childcare might also improve the variety and quality of children's lives. In the accounts presented here, the role of the childcare itself has been neutral or positive: children are no worse off for spending time in childcare, and (according to their parents) somewhat better off during the remaining time with their parents.

THE STRESS OF CHILDCARE ARRANGEMENTS

The section above discussed the terms in which the transition to employment and using childcare can be justified by parents. This justification may evaporate if the arrangements do not materialise as expected. The child may react badly to separation. If the quality of the child's environment deteriorates because the quality of the chosen source declines, because the source is withdrawn or a new combination of sources becomes necessary, then the equation may no longer balance in favour of taking up work. For parents too, arranging childcare around work may prove more strenuous than expected, and alter the balance of the equation.

Eileen associated her earlier nervous breakdown with problems arranging childcare.

It was childminders and childminding. Everything to do with [my son], because he was really clingy and upset. When he went into hospital this last time, I just thought 'Right that's it. I want to spend more time with [him] rather than working, while he's a baby'. Like in the morning I was just getting up, rushing about with him, taking him somewhere, coming home and then rushing about with him, giving him his tea and everything and then putting him to bed. So really I had no time.

If childcare arrangements were complicated or unreliable, parents could spend their restricted time with their children hastily organising temporary arrangements. Parents spoke of the stress this caused, the antithesis of 'quality' time.

I have to do a lot of juggling in my own life. So it's always constantly on your mind, trying to arrange things all the time. It's quite stressful knowing when she's sick, I've got to take another day off work, that type of thing. You've got to juggle everything. I wouldn't advise it. It's hard work. [Sue]

If it was worrying from day to day, I don't think I could have lasted this long. 'Cos it's more hassle than it's worth really, having to run from person to person. [Sandra]

Thus lone mothers who effect a balance which favours taking up work, once there may find it is a *fine* balance. Any minor changes in childcare or work circumstances can make the situation physically or financially untenable. As Sian explained.

You think 'Wow, he's got a place at nursery' and nursery finishes at half past eleven. What do you do with them at half past eleven? The sheer business of: you then have to get a child from the nursery to whatever other arrangement you've made. When you are not in a situation where you can repay that. You can't say 'You do it on Monday and I'll do it on Tuesday' because you are supposed to be working. So you end up having to pay somebody to take the child from the nursery to somewhere else. [Sian]

I never had time to do anything. Not really. All I seemed to be doing was getting up, working, and coming home, and going to sleep! [Maxine]

SUMMARY

Lone mothers seeking work have to align two moving targets: the availability of suitable childcare and an acceptable job opportunity. The targets had to align chronologically and financially. Parents outlined the principles underlying this process. They would need to balance the value of their final income and time remaining each week for the family to be together against their out-of-work income and the quality of the time spent at home. The decision could be simplified by awarding priority to one or other component of the work entry equation: childcare or employment opportunity. Parents would fix the more restricted element before finalising the more flexible element. The final combination should increase the value of a family's time together to such an extent that losses are outweighed. A positive balance would favour taking up work. Problems organising or sustaining childcare will draw the balance away from favouring employment.

This is an idealised statement of principles. Parents' decisions can be explained in the context of such principles but each individual will bring different priorities to bear on different circumstances making any one decision difficult to predict. Parents make decisions about work with imperfect knowledge. They may not know themselves how much difference an increase in income will make to their lives, let alone their children's. Work entry demands a whole new set of behaviours which offer a different set of rewards and drawbacks for the lone mother from those she experiences out of work. Often the only way to find out whether a combination of work and childcare is tenable, let alone preferable, is to try it. The complexity of the decision-making process, the effort required to get it right, and the risks of getting it wrong and the harsher consequences of such an error, all must put some parents off the attempt completely.

Chapter 8

CHILDCARE COSTS AND AFFORDABILITY

This report has been careful to differentiate discussion of childcare costs (in pounds and pence) from that of its affordability (a judgement specific to the lone parent family and a specific job opportunity). Chapter 2 showed something of the costs, but affordability is a judgement made in the context of each opportunity considered. The two are related: affordability is how the lone parent translates the observed or anticipated cost in a specific context. But in evaluating the likelihood of work entry, it is affordability which determines whether or not a childcare source is used.

A further dimension is value for money. In a limited budget, more expensive childcare will only be sought if it offers some advantage, in convenience, quality or flexibility, over cheaper care. Some parents spoke of their reluctance to use free or low cost care provided by relatives because of the obligation it places on them to reciprocate. Others described childcare situations which could physically threaten or upset their children. Such sources carry a social cost which exceeds their utility, particularly in comparison with other care which may a carry larger financial cost.

Childcare is of course evaluated on many other criteria besides its affordability (Chapter 5). Childcare costs can only be compared in the abstract when like is compared with like: the same hours, the same standards of care and similarly accessible location. In practice parents have few such opportunities: sources will always differ in some way. Parents must weigh up the social and financial gains and losses from each acceptable source available to them. This evaluation by parents ties in to the overall balancing act of matching childcare to job opportunities discussed in Chapter 7.

Once again, of course, the imperfect knowledge of parents must be taken into account. Parents may generalise about the availability of both work and childcare and about how well they can meet their childcare needs from an anticipated wage and benefit income.

Parents were presented with job scenarios against which they were asked to assess their childcare costs in Chapter 4. Some chose different sources of childcare when faced with differing financial returns from working. For most who would vary their childcare in this way, they would seek as good a source of childcare as they felt they could afford. Care which comes at a higher price was not essential to tip the equation in favour of employment. For these parents childcare was a consumption good in its own right, not simply a means to a better income. In more than one instance, however, childcare costs became less of a barrier when parents were presented with the better-paid job. One parent quoted a childcare cost for the second job scenario which was half that she quoted for the first job (with the same hours). One interpretation is simply that she exaggerated how much more affordable childcare becomes with a better-paid job. A second is that childcare cost is a legitimised reason among lone mothers for refusing unattractive job opportunities.

If the second interpretation is true, then we must be careful in taking parents' discussions of cost at face value. Much more important is how these discussions reflect on parents' interpretations of the affordability of childcare.

THE 'AFFORDABILITY' OF PAID-FOR CHILDCARE

Childcare costs are fixed, but wage rates and hours of work will vary from job to job. Thus the affordability of childcare is specific to the job opportunity and the childcare it necessitates. In the absence of a job offer, parents can only comment on the affordability of care if they make assumptions about their wages in work and the types of childcare they will need. Parents are only too aware of how well- or ill-equipped they are to enter the labour market. Some will view childcare as unaffordable because they feel the work they are likely to get will never permit them to buy the childcare they will need and leave a sufficient final income to make the whole venture worthwhile. Parents who make such assumptions, like Maggie, will say they 'cannot afford childcare' and will restrict their job search to work which is unlikely to require paid childcare.

> *I would like to be able to earn and have more money; but if it means working and not having more money there is no point in me working. 'Cos then I have to worry about childcare as well. 'Cos the kids are at school at nine and they come out at 3.15. So I can only work a short day anyway. Then I'd pay someone to pick my children up and I can't see myself earning enough money to also pay someone. I'm not going to come out with any more money.*

Parents were asked to give the best estimate of the actual cost of the childcare available to them. Estimates varied considerably from £0 to £70 depending on the parents' circumstances and locality. Given that some parents had access to 'free' childcare, this level of variation in perceived childcare cost accounts for some of the variation in the attractiveness with which work was viewed. For example, Julie would pay her cousins £5 each week to look after her children, if she could get an employer to take her on. Childcare cost is not what keeps her out of the labour market.

Some parents, such as Sarah, also had to pay a retainer for weeks they did not use the care, which added to the overall cost. Tracy continued to work and use 'unaffordable' childcare in order to retain her childcare place.

> *It's only a temporary job, so the money's rubbish. I actually pay my childminder half what I earn ... It's not really helping me, it's just trying to keep the childminding place open*

Sandra felt more distant from the paid childcare market. Like Tracy, she assessed the affordability of childcare in terms of how much of her wages she was prepared to spare to pay for care. The amount would be too low, she felt, to recompense formal carers.

> *I don't think I could afford to pay for a professional childminder. 'Cos I'd hate to be handing over all my wages at the end of the week. 'Cos I don't earn enough for that. Rates I pay – some people are offering – they would be working for nothing.*

Sandra was able to use her parents to cover the hours she worked either side of the school day. Her childcare was thus financially 'affordable' but she felt guilty about her reliance on them. Other lone mothers, such as Marie, were reluctant to use relatives and so placed themselves in a position where they had to pay for care.

> *I don't think anybody should be helping. I think you should be getting a wage good enough to be able to pay it yourself.* [Marie]

For lone mothers, all childcare carried some cost, whether it was provided by family, friends or professionals. The cost of paid-for care could be unaffordable because its financial cost exceeded likely financial resources. The affordability of 'free' care could be judged in a parallel way against a parent's emotional or human resources.

The 'Affordability' of Unpaid Care

Unpaid care carried out by friends and relatives carries a social cost: producing a debt of gratitude or a requirement for some form of reciprocal activity. For some parents this price was also too high to justify movement into work requiring use of such care.

> *You end up working 39 hours a week or whatever yourself and then when you get home you want a bit of time with your kids, you find that you're looking after other people's children.* [Ruth]

Maggie preferred the idea of a reciprocal arrangement. This restricted the hours of work she was prepared to consider. She said she would prefer a three day a week job.

> *...then I've still got two days a week to sort of pay somebody back.*

For a variety of reasons, parents could find the exchange of cash inappropriate when friends or relatives cared for children. Monetary exchange could interfere with benefit or tax status, and set amounts of money might seem unsuitable for arrangements which are informal and non-contractual in nature. As an alternative, reciprocal care might not be practicable. Recompense between parent and carer might then take the form of a gift.

> *If she does babysit, I'll get her a packet of cigs.* [Elizabeth]

Most often the gift took the form of a packet of cigarettes. As Melanie pointed out, this did not necessarily result in a cheap form of childcare.

> *If I have to nip anywhere now, she'll have to take the kids. I'll just buy some cigs 'cos I'm only gone an hour, but that's still £2.67 just for nipping out for an hour.*

Other parents who were out of work 'paid' for childcare in this way, whenever they needed to be apart from their children. When Carrie needed to visit the hospital:

> *It doesn't just cost the bus fare. It's like an hour and a half there, an hour and a half back. So I have to find someone for [my daughter] from school, because she can't be left. I won't get home till like seven at night. So I have to find someone for [my daughter] for school, usually a friend. It only usually costs me like 40 cigarettes*

Informal and technically 'unpaid' childcare could thus engender costs, either financial in the purchase of gifts or through the exchange of time and effort (in a form of 'reciprocity'). Some felt these arrangements preferable to paying for formal childcare: they offered greater flexibility and reinforced social interactions. However, the non-contractual nature of such arrangements meant some parents were less comfortable with them.

> *I'm not very good at asking favours, to be honest. That's what I said about independence. I don't like asking anyone for anything!* [May]

Arrangements based on 'favours' could in practice resemble paid childcare in all but name.

> *I pay her £30 a month. Yeah, I give her childcare money. Because I feel she's doing me a favour.* [Sophie]

Childcare is used for a number of purposes, but this study concentrates on its role as a route into work. Parents who find work and have pre-school age children, and those who have only school-age children but whose job continues beyond school hours, need childcare. For the childcare to enable rather than hinder work entry, its costs – interpreted financially and socially – must not detract excessively from the gains work offers the parent and her family. Childcare which achieves this condition is affordable, that which does not is unaffordable.

The equation lone mothers have been trying to balance carries financial and non-financial elements on both sides. A particular job opportunity will offer job satisfaction, possible career progression, a new social environment and the benefits and disadvantages of the family's separation. It will also offer a wage and demand a time commitment which must be matched by a form of childcare the parent and children find acceptable. Different types of care may aid the children's education or socialisation to different degrees, and others may worsen it. Thus some care will offer better value than others. The cost of this care may be financial or social, paid in reciprocal activity or incurring a debt of gratitude. The role of the social cost is also important in evaluating the impact of the disregard below.

The financial calculation must, of course, balance. Childcare costs in excess of disposable income are not sustainable for long, and parents are likely to want some improvement in standards of living in exchange for their effort of working. But this is only part of the story. The financial and social gains from work and any gains for the children in using childcare must outweigh the costs of the childcare, other in-work costs and the loss of time the family has together. Parents might also seek compensation for their efforts in arranging childcare.

The affordability of childcare is judged from how well this multi-component equation can be made to balance. The childcare disregard has been designed to tip the balance each week by up to £38.20[1] more in favour of work entry. How lone parents interpret its likely effect is explored in the second half of this chapter.

THE CHILDCARE DISREGARD

One recent policy initiative designed to make lone parents and some couples better able to work and afford childcare is the 'childcare disregard'. The initiative (described fully in Chapter 4) at the time of the study resulted in up to £38.20 of the first £40 of earnings spent on childcare each week being returned to the claimant in the form of increased eligibility for Family Credit, Housing

Benefit and Council Tax Benefit. From April 1996, the amount of the disregard has been increased to £60. How much of the income spent on childcare is 'retained' depends on the benefits claimed in work and the level of earnings, maintenance and other income received.

In order to qualify for the disregard, lone parents must work 16 hours a week or more and pay a professional, registered carer for a child under the age of 11 years. The childcare must be provided by formal sources: a registered childminder, nursery or after-school club; or an out-of-hours or holiday play scheme provided by a local authority or school.

In practice, because Family Credit is paid for six months before a new claim is required, the term-time and holiday costs are averaged out to produce an annual estimate of the cost of childcare. The Family Credit calculation assumes 1/52 of this estimate is paid each week.

The disregard was introduced in October 1994, at the time the National Survey was entering the field. Considerable publicity was associated with the launch. Despite the very short period between introduction and the National Survey, six in ten lone parents had heard of the 'help with childcare charges from social security'. Most (three-quarters of those who had heard) had seen television adverts and 11 per cent had seen newspaper or magazine coverage.

Awareness was only slightly lower among those who would be entitled to it were they to move into work. Some 57 per cent of lone parents of children aged ten years or younger and not working 16 or more hours each week had heard of the disregard. If the further restriction that parents must also be prepared to use and have available formal childcare of the types eligible for the disregard is applied (32 per cent of lone parents not working 16 or more hours), 55 per cent of the 'client group' were aware of the disregard.

Knowledge of the disregard

Interviewers were instructed not to introduce the subject of the disregard until the end of the depth interviews. Respondents were asked first what they knew of the scheme. Interviewers explained the disregard to those who were not fully aware. Respondents were asked what they thought its effects would be for them.

For the disregard to make a difference, parents would need to be aware of its existence, and of its effects on their likely income in work. They would need some idea of its financial value. In practice the amount would not be fixed, but some typical values were in circulation, and positively received.

> *It was on the budget saying there would be help for working parents who have their children in childcare. So it makes people go back to work, if you will. So there is help, but I've never used it so I don't know. Some folk say it were about thirty pound to help you towards your costs but I don't know. That isn't too bad that.* [Jenny]

Once the disregard had been explained, Mary, previously pessimistic about her employment prospects, went further.

> *Well that just changes my whole view on everything that I've just said ... so that makes a big difference 'cos you couldn't afford to give that out your wages.*

Since the amount could vary according to the benefits claimed and the amount paid for childcare, parents could have difficulty assessing its worth. Specific forms of childcare taken up to enable employment yielding wages within a particular range – in combination with claims for certain benefits – result in a fraction of childcare costs being 'refunded'. In effect the scheme was another moving target to be taken into account when matching job vacancies and available childcare.

> *The minute that you earn enough to go out to work to pay for childminding facilities you're too far up the threshold for Family Credit. So catch-22 isn't it?* [Sharon]

It should make certain childcare plus work combinations more favourable, but parents might have difficulty understanding which these were.

Rebecca was an ideal candidate to benefit from the disregard, but she found the scheme very complicated to understand.

> *As far as I could I tell, from the way that the advert was worded the government were going to give you money to go out to work. You*

know they were actually going to pay some childminding fees. But, after reading it, it was that they weren't actually giving you anything. They were just going to make some form of allowance on your supposed income, so in fact you weren't actually getting anything towards your childcare. It really, well like I say the way that I read it, it didn't really make a lot of sense.

Lone parents find it difficult to predict their likely income from means-tested benefits in work (Marsh and McKay, 1993b). Few know the size of the taper or the amounts of benefit they are likely to receive. Because the childcare disregard is intimately imbedded in this system, it is vulnerable to the same levels of misunderstanding.

They're offering to give you money towards paying them, that's as much as I know. I don't know how much this is, whether they actually give you the going rate for what they're paying, or whether you've got to put the rest too. [Marie]

And at the time of interview, full details of eligibility had yet to filter through.

If you want to go back to work you can have £38 or something ... don't really know much about it. Whether it's just for Income Support people doing so many hours a week. [June]

Once again, one way to find out was to experiment.

My mum's a registered childminder ... At the moment they've brought out this new thing that you can claim for childminder money, so I'm going to try for that as well. 'Cos I give like my mum £20 and my auntie, so it's still money for childminding really. I'll try and see what happens. Probably won't get any. [Tanya]

If Tanya was successful then she would have substituted some of the social cost of her childcare (her indebtedness to her mother and aunt) with a financial cost she no longer had to meet. May, out of work at the time of interview, thought along similar lines.

It would be more of a sort of a business-like arrangement where I'd be paying her to do something. And if I was getting help to do that, it would be a big incentive, 'cos it's going back to what I keep saying about me not liking to ask anybody favours. So if I was getting help to get a businesslike arrangement with someone, where I was paying them: yes, that would be it.

Thus the substitution of informal with formal care could alleviate some of the anxieties parents had about work. The disregard would make it easier for people like May to adopt the contractual relationship they sought with their source of childcare. Tanya might also feel more comfortable staying in work under the disregard. But each substitution of payments for formally 'free' care of the type Tanya proposes could imply some dead weight cost for the scheme, since expenditure would not engender new movement into work. Many mothers will not qualify because the childcare they intend to use is not covered by the scheme.

I don't see why you've got to use a registered childminder and ... they don't do the hours and weekends. I mean these people have got to have my kids Saturday lunchtime and Sunday lunchtime, from half ten in the morning until about half three in the afternoon. [Cynth]

When you claim Family Credit now they say they give you so much towards your childminder, but then they've got to be a registered childminder. So if I was to get more hours at the club and work nights, I don't think you can get a registered childminder that'll come and sit here till like half past twelve at night. [Elizabeth]

Some parents' and children's preferences for informal childcare were explored in Chapter 6. The same issues arose again in the context of the disregard. A substantial minority preferred using friends and relatives, and often anticipated paying them.

It's a lot more flexible. It's just better all round, really. And if you could pay your relatives for doing it, somebody more trustworthy than a stranger, a strange childminder. [Alison]

The scheme is intended to reduce one of the barriers to work entry and to make it easier for those in work to stay there. The scheme may not be viewed as effective if expenditure is directed towards parents who were in work and were likely to stay there anyway (some of whom may have been drawn into scope of Family Credit simply by the disregard), or to those who would anyway have used free sources of childcare. Such expenditure could be regarded as a 'dead weight' cost. The restriction to formal sources may have been intended to avoid the extent of dead weight cost – payments to relatives who would have cared for free. However, the scheme can also be viewed as less effective if these restrictions inhibit lone mothers who would only enter work if they could use friends or relatives.

Lone parents' response to two aspects of the restrictions on childcare sources need to be assessed before the effectiveness of the disregard can be evaluated. The first is who among parents would prefer to pay for care which is not covered by the scheme? The second is who among these will choose to substitute formal care for informal care in order to qualify for the disregard?

This study cannot estimate answers to these questions. Interviews took place too soon after the introduction of the scheme for parents to be sufficiently aware of its implications. Those not in work might be considering entering work using childcare for the first time, making it difficult to discern their likely sources before the introduction of the disregard.

Many parents are likely to prefer to pay in cash for a formerly free source of childcare if this displaces some or all of the social cost (such as reciprocal obligations).

> *I'll have to pay for proper care if I get Family Credit and I have to get somebody to watch the kids. But it's got to be a proper one, where I could just get a friend to watch them and then pay them, it's got to be a proper childminder. Now the cheapest childminder is fifty pound a week. So I've got to get extra money coming in from somewhere.* [Melanie]

Melanie has also highlighted a problem at the transition stage of moving in to work. The barrier posed by start-up costs to work entry have been referred to elsewhere (Marsh, Ford and Finlayson, 1996 forthcoming). In addition to meeting new in-work costs, parents may need new clothes and sources of transport. If paid childcare needs to be used from the outset, to qualify for the disregard in Family Credit, then an additional cost is attached to the transition. Parents may not now wait long for their claim to be processed, but costs will still have to be met, often up front, which will only be recompensed later in Family Credit or wages. Some parents may be considerably daunted by the need to finance the transition. Chapter 7 has shown that the transition is a risky time anyway, as parents try to match work and childcare arrangements. The risk may be enhanced if paid childcare is used from the outset in that there is no guarantee that the benefit claim will be successful.

Some mothers were unhappy at their current or imminent exclusion from the client group because of their children's ages. As explained in Chapter 6, the majority of parents felt their children needed supervision to age 13 years.

Are 11 year-olds suddenly OK to be latchkey children? That's very suspect. Boredom and lack of supervision: they don't know. They can be sensible a lot of the time but they're not grown-ups and they still do need supervision. [Sian]

Also, parents of children with disabilities would need care which extended into teenage and beyond. But as the problem was more one of availability of suitable care, at a cost within reach of a working lone parent, the extension of the disregard solely to this group would be unlikely to bring about a major shift into employment. Parents with older disabled children tended to have been caring for their children, out of the labour market, for many years, and defined their life roles in such terms. For most such parents, the cost of childcare was not the major issue.

Experience of using the disregard

Depth interviews were undertaken in the early months of 1995, too early for many lone mothers to have experience of claiming the disregard. One respondent who knew she had benefited from it was Sarah. She faced the situation explained in Chapter 4 whereby her childcare expenses were taken into account in her Housing Benefit claim. Her experience unearthed some administrative teething troubles.

I pay the childminder and the cost gets taken into account with your Housing Benefit claim. But, having said that, we've just had a new Housing Benefit claim. You have to fill it out each year. On the form, there's nothing to say about childcare. In October, when it started, I went to the council, and said 'What's happening about the childcare? Is there any way that it does affect my Housing Benefit?' and she said 'Yes, but you have to get a letter from your child-minder, saying that she's registered and they have to write to us, and tell us how much you pay.' Now, if I hadn't have asked, I wouldn't have known.

The process of claiming the disregard is somewhat easier for Family Credit claimants as a pro forma declaration by the childminder or nursery manager is included in the Family Credit claim pack.

Respondents' views on the disregard

When asked to assess a new scheme about which they knew little, lone mothers tended to err on the side of pessimism. Some potential users of childcare who had heard of the disregard were not impressed with the amount of childcare cost it would cover. Marsha had given up work when her free source of childcare, her mother, had moved out of the area.

It's not very good. It's something like £28 a week, it's pathetic ... Like me at the time now, I'm just sat on me arse doing nothing and nobody's telling me to go to work. I think they should do a scheme where they actually can sort out childminding. 'Cos as it is I'm on Income Support. I'll get no money for childminding. So then you've got to work out whether it's worth going to work to begin with 'cos of all the benefits you lose. [Marsha]

I still don't think it would be enough. It's about £24 a week. No, I don't think that. That's not enough really is it? They can charge anything can't they? [Margaret]

Since, at the time of interview, the disregard covered only the first £40 spent by each *parent* on childcare, not on each child, the more children parents had the less of their childcare cost was likely to be met through the disregard.

That would cover one child but if you've got two or three it's no way. [Cynth]

> *I don't think as I stand now I could ever work full-time because even with the extra help you can get it's only forty pound and it'd never cover a childminder for three of them.* [Elaine]

The problem was related to that of availability, since parents whose three children could all use the same source were likely to incur lower costs than those requiring a separate source for each child.

Adequacy of the disregard

How realistic is it for lone parents to criticise the level of the disregard? Some 38 per cent of full-time working lone parents pay for childcare (Finlayson, Ford and Marsh, 1996). Their mean childcare cost is £35.28 (median £30) per week. Only a third who pay, pay £41 or more each week. At face value, then, most lone parents should not find a £40 disregard too low. But this assumption overlooks the childcare costs those out of work face, since they do not contribute to the figures.

Of those lone mothers interviewed in the National Survey who were not working 16 or more hours but who expected to use childcare if they did so, two-thirds expected to have to pay for the care they used at a mean cost of just over £40. Half expected to pay more than £40, and this may explain some perceptions of inadequacy in the level of the childcare disregard. Among the client group most able to take advantage of the disregard – those with a child aged under 11 years who had available, acceptable formal sources of childcare – the figures were much the same. Four in five expected to pay for any childcare they used at a mean cost of £40 (median £40). So a considerable proportion contemplating paying for childcare would come within scope of the disregard.

There were few among the client group who, if they qualified for the disregard at all, would see little benefit. Only 20 per cent who expected to pay thought their childcare bill would exceed £56. It would thus still be possible for 80 per cent of these parents to receive at least half (and from April 1996, the majority) of their childcare expenses in the form of Family Credit, not to mention additional Housing Benefit or Council Tax Benefit. The proportion would decline to two-thirds if they chose to pay for their *preferred* source of childcare.

A majority should see considerable benefit from the disregard – if they qualify at all. Equally though, a minority who anticipate high childcare costs see the disregard making only a minor contribution.

> *I think they pay a maximum of £26 a week towards childcare, but childcare is £90 a week, if you've got a young one ... it's £90 minimum in [this town] for a childminder ... from eight till five.* [Ellie]

Do lone parents benefit from the disregard?

Parents will only benefit from the disregard if they qualify. To explain why some low earners will not qualify requires an explanation of the mechanics of Family Credit. Family Credit is paid to those in work of 16 hours or more whose independent income (earnings, maintenance, notional income from savings) falls below a specified *upper* threshold, based on family size and ages. The amount of Family Credit paid is fixed if independent income is so low as to fall below a *lower* threshold. The amount received is the maximum Family Credit payment available to a particular family. Above this lower threshold, this amount is reduced by 70p for every extra pound in independent income.

So some will not qualify for Family Credit because their independent income exceeds the upper threshold, even after the first £40 of earnings (£60 from 1996) spent on childcare has been ignored. Others will see no increase in the amount of Family Credit entitlement because their independent income was so low as to qualify them for maximum Family Credit even before childcare costs were taken into account. They would receive the same amount of benefit regardless. The disregard may result in higher levels of Housing Benefit and Council Tax Benefit payment but only for those liable for rent and Council Tax, respectively.

SUMMARY OF POLICY IMPLICATIONS

The childcare disregard was greeted positively by a number of the lone parents who were aware of it. At a level of £40, it would accommodate the childcare costs of half those out of work who expected to pay for care when working 16 hours or more. At a level of £60 it will accommodate the costs of 90 per cent. Few anticipated costs so high that they were out of the scope of the scheme. There are, however, three other areas of its implementation which raise most concern.

Knowledge and structure of the scheme

Although the level of awareness of the disregard was high at an early stage of its implementation, 45 per cent of those most able to benefit had not heard of it in Autumn 1994. For the benefit to have any effect on these parents' consideration of employment, they need to know not only that it exists, but that it can apply to them. One method would be through a repeated awareness campaign. Television had proved by far the most successful medium in 1994.

Some parents also needed a clearer idea of how the disregard worked, and particularly of its likely value to them. A clear understanding is essential if lone mothers are to come somewhere close to a reasoned calculation in weighing up the gains and losses from employment. This is a complex process with many variables. Parents might find it easier to assess the value of working if they knew that 100 per cent of costs below £40 would be refunded. But then lone mothers would have little incentive to seek cheaper suppliers. Childcare providers might also raise prices to the nominal limit of £40. A clear argument exists to favour funding a proportion of the costs of care below 100 per cent. It would nonetheless prove easier for parents to calculate if that proportion is fixed, say at 90 per cent of the first £40, than for the 'refund' to vary between 0 and 96 per cent of the costs. This would also remove the anomaly of renters and council tax payers being able to reclaim more of the cost.

Payment of a fixed proportion of childcare costs for those earning within Family Credit thresholds would also extend additional help for childcare to those who need it most: those whose earnings are so low that under the present system they qualify for maximum Family Credit both before and after their childcare costs have been taken into account. It may tempt into work those with most problems supplying enough hours.

Restrictions on the age of children eligible

Six in ten lone parents would want to use childcare for a 13 year-old child. Extension of the scheme to cover care for parents whose youngest is aged 11, 12 or 13 years would enable parents of older children to enter or continue work which extends beyond school hours. It would also help those parents of older children with disabilities, where affordable care was available. As reported in Chapter 6, the problem for parents working and using childcare for children of these ages is convincing the child of the need for supervision. It is unlikely that parents would extend care to cover older children if they did not consider it necessary. The children would simply reject it. A high dead weight cost seems unlikely.

Restrictions on sources of childcare

This is the most difficult problem to resolve. To extend its client base, either parents need to be persuaded to use the formal sources recognised, or the disregard must become available for a wider range of sources. Parents who are unwilling to use formal childcare do so for several reasons: fear of strangers – often generated by unrepresentative media portrayal or hearsay; rejection of formal provision by the children themselves; feelings that known carers offer a better understanding of or form of care for their children; the perceived cost differential between formal and informal sources; the need for out-of-hours or flexible childcare to match irregular working hours. Each of these concerns must be dealt with in turn.

Fear of strangers caring for children cannot be quickly eliminated. Nor is it an issue which can be sidelined. Unlike parents in couples, lone parents have sole responsibility for their children, most of whom have lost their other parent through a distressing separation. Lone parents may be understandably reluctant to place themselves apart from their children for extended periods. If this separation requires the child to leave familiar settings and people for a different caring environment and unknown carer, then the reluctance is even more understandable. It will be overcome only if the parent and child feel comfortable with the source of care. There are many examples of children initially rejecting care they later accepted. Familiarity can develop, but the initial steps will be difficult. These could be eased if the parent could remain present for initial sessions. A parallel is the transition to school. Nearly all parents are prepared to trust their children to 'strangers' in the education system. Familiarity with the concept and universality of the experience must play a part. Although commonly accepted by parents, children often need considerable support in school for the first few days.

Childcare is not compulsory, and is far from being a universal experience in the social environments many lone parent families inhabit. Any measures which increase the exposure of communities containing lone parents to childcare will increase familiarity with the process. Children often want to go to childcare simply because that is where their friends are (Smith, 1995). Media could also be used to portray a more representative or positive image of childcare.

Some parents described how they had arranged initially to be present in childcare settings themselves, or had eased their fears through trial runs and random checks. These processes take time and can cost money. In the first days of a new job, the parent will not have the time, and beforehand she is unlikely to have the money. Providers of childcare might be encouraged to offer free care on trial.

If in the lone parent's estimation, friends and relatives offer better care than other sources, parents could encourage them to register as childminders with their local authority.

The cost differential between formal and informal care may form an important part of parents' attachment to informal sources. But the differential is, of course, eroded by the disregard. As the working of the disregard becomes better understood, so the strength of this reason should diminish. Likewise, parents may come to prefer subsidised formal sources since provision is contractual and carries a lower social cost or obligation to reciprocal activity. A factor less often emphasised was the flexibility of payment for informal methods. Parents may be better able to postpone or stagger payments to match tight budget demands if the childcare provider is a friend or relative. These preferences may be stronger among those who feel less comfortable negotiating with formal or institutionalised structures. Again, childcare providers might find it advantageous to increase custom through budget and flexible payment schemes.

Finally, formal sources might find it hard to rival the flexibility of informal sources. Friends and relatives might be available at short notice and at all hours, in line with the demands of the jobs many lone parents might be able to take. Among the 21 workers in the depth study, shift-work, lunchtime and evening catering and bar work, early morning and late evening cleaning all featured alongside more regular weekday hours.

Most formal care is not designed with parents' working hours in mind. Some is – notably after school clubs and private nurseries/crèches – and hours can extend from as early as 6.30 in the morning to 7 at night. Such care comes at a high hourly rate, and still fails to cover evening, weekend and night work. If shift-working parents were not able to use informal sources, the only formal care sources would be nannies or au pairs for whom lone parent families are unlikely to have the room or be able to meet the fees.

The problem is one of demand. While lone parents need childcare to do such work, women in couples often do not, because their partner is home from his daytime job. So few people need evening and night time care that the critical mass needed to make a service available (or less expensive) is not there.

Another problem is that although working parents may have demands on their waking hours which vary from week to week, children have fairly regular routines. Parents would prefer them to be in their own beds in their own homes at the same time each night even if they cannot be there to see to it themselves. Friends, relatives and babysitters can fulfil this function, but few formal carers could provide this service.

The solution may rest in making informal services eligible for the disregard to cover certain hours of work, or types of work. Employers may need to certify that such demands will be made of their lone parent employees.

The policy implications of the childcare disregard extend beyond those of social security. It is a means of reducing dependence on benefits. But it is one which depends on childcare being available. It may increase childcare demand, and increase the proportion of Britain's children who experience childcare. There are implications for education, employment, health, fiscal policy and local government. In consequence, the concerns with the scheme touch upon the activities of many Government departments and agencies. The wide range of measures needed to lower fully the childcare barrier for lone parents cannot be implemented by one department alone.

Note

1   The disregard on childcare costs permits a maximum additional return in benefit from £40 spent on childcare each week of £38.20. The majority (£28) would be received in additional Family Credit, plus £7.80 additional Housing Benefit and £2.40 more Council Tax Benefit.

Chapter 9

CONCLUSIONS

The decision to seek paid work or remain at home is a complicated one for lone parents, and not one determined solely by the
availability or cost of childcare. The issue of childcare generally, or
even the effect of an initiative such as a disregard on certain childcare costs, cannot be understood except in the broader context
within which lone parents make this decision. Whilst work can
bring long-term monetary, social and emotional rewards, it can
pose risks to family cohesion and income security. The advantages
and disadvantages of life in work must be weighed up against the
benefits and drawbacks of life out of work. Each chapter of this
study has focused on a different element of this equation which
must be balanced if paid work is to find favour.

Lone parents find (or place) themselves at a wide range of dis-
tances from the work entry equation: some distant from considering the logistics of taking up work, others close. The most distant
are those who simply cannot contemplate working. It is worth
remembering that although the long-term sick were not interviewed for the depth study, a steadily increasing proportion of
lone parents report themselves as suffering from a long-term or
limiting illness[1] and nearly half of these – one in seven lone
parents – feel that their health problems make it more difficult for
them to get or keep paid work. A similar proportion have sick or
disabled children whom, for the time being, they feel unable to
leave.

The family circumstances of other lone parents also make work
very difficult. As the average duration of lone parenthood is about
five years, at any one time the population contains many who have
only recently become lone parents. They need time to adapt to
their new circumstances and will stay out of the labour market

while they do so. Adaptation will take longer for some than others and some may never fully adjust before they repartner or their children grow up. For women to take up work while remaining a lone mother, children, who have already been separated from their father, must also accept separation from their mother for extended periods.

Others, who prior to lone parenthood were among the three in ten women with partners and who were 'economically inactive', may wish to continue the same role in their partner's absence. They will simply continue looking after home and family as they did before. Single, never-partnered lone parents, new to parenthood, may simply be following a traditional role model represented by their own mother when they choose to stay at home with their children. Many lone mothers define their lives in terms of their child-rearing and homemaking roles.

Still others who once worked may find that, in the absence of another partner, they need to spend more time with their children and cannot reconcile their caring role with paid work. Likewise, the departure of the partner may focus the burden of other non-remunerative tasks, such as looking after the home or caring for elderly relatives, more acutely on the remaining parent's potential work time.

In order to work, lone mothers must subject themselves and their families' economic future to the vagaries of the labour market and a market wage which values their skills as a worker not as a mother or homemaker. A low skills base and work inexperience may result in a lower valuation in work than out. They may find it difficult to find a vacancy which matches their skills. Low earnings potential in the labour market will mean in-work costs, which need to be purchased from a market open to all parents, seem all the more expensive. If the mother aspires to a high quality child-rearing role (which she is likely to do) the relative value for money offered by paid-for care will seem low. She is unlikely to understand sufficiently the system of tapers and thresholds applicable to the in-work benefits which can be applied to her earnings. She will be comparing a known level of out-of-work income with an unknown (and difficult to predict) level of in-work income. The equation evaluating costs and benefits in and out of work is likely to remain weighted to favour the secure child-rearing environment and guaranteed income out of work. Thus, even in the presence of severe hardship, and regardless of the incentives to improve income offered by paid work, it must be accepted that at least some lone parents will not be motivated or able to work for at least some of the time they spend as lone parents.

RECONCILING WORK AND PARENTING ROLES

Not all lone mothers feel that using childcare is compatible with their perceptions of what is best for themselves and their children. Yet this is a prerequisite of entering work with hours which overlap with time the mother would otherwise spend caring. In other words, in using childcare she should not feel she is reneging on her caring role, or at least she should feel that her work is providing something else of equal value to her child, such as a better standard of living or simply a happier mother. This is achieved either by locating care she feels is at least of a quality comparable to her own, or by balancing the shortfall in care the children experience while she is at work by using the financial returns from work to improve the quality of the remaining time the family has together. Ideally, the family would seek both, but to the extent that better quality care costs more, there is a trade-off between using income to enhance the childcare or the time the family is together. The equation will balance if the lone parent can command a sufficiently high wage to be able to substitute for and enhance her own caring role in such a way that the net improvement in the care the children receive is positive. Thus, the availability of *suitable* childcare should increase the motivation to work. In rural areas childcare may simply be scarce, and even in urban areas low-cost childcare places will be limited. Parents also hold strong views on the types of care they consider suitable. Whether or not the parent is able to afford such childcare takes the argument back to incentives.

This study has been concerned with the 'cost' of childcare and its affect on lone parents' ability to work. Although the literal meaning of cost (how many pounds need to be paid out for different kinds of provision) has been considered in some detail, it has become clear that different kinds of childcare place different demands on parents and their ability to work, on children and the family relationship which are measured in non-financial terms. Some forms of childcare provided 'free' by friends and relatives are based on immediate or long-term reciprocity within the family or community. Other forms of childcare may exact a price on the children's independence or on the parental bond.

Of course, like work, the use of childcare can bring other, non-financial benefits, such as enhancing the educational development of the child. Many parents use childcare to enhance their own parenting and not just, if at all, to permit them to go out to work. Edwards (1993) has posed the question thus 'Is childcare for lone mothers to work or do lone mothers work for daycare?'. Parents must weigh up the benefits and disadvantages for their family of using daycare in place of their own parenting, and the benefits and disadvantages to their family of going out to work. Parents are balancing net outcomes of two processes: substituting for some of their own time spent parenting *and* their own entry into the labour market. The use of childcare can be undertaken and justified independently of the work entry. Because work entry is dependent on childcare, it requires justification of both processes.

Some of the positive and negative consequences of balancing this duality of roles in parenthood, gleaned from the parents' perspective in interviews, were illustrated in Figure 3.1. As children grow older, the balance of roles is made easier by the intervention of compulsory schooling. Spending time apart from children is no longer optional, and for the duration of school hours, the decision to enter work becomes one-dimensional, based only on the net benefits of work. Outside of school hours, the dual balance remains.

As children grow older, they too become entitled to a judgement about the acceptability of childcare. Children will wish to become more independent of their parents and thus deny their parents the option of spending time with them. Alternatively they may reject certain types of care provision. In both situations, parents must weigh up their responsibilities with the net benefits of working to decide the best course of action.

In most circumstances, lone parents will bear sole responsibility for any decision to change the family's status quo. Given the complexity of the decision, and the far-reaching consequences of the outcomes, they are likely to vacillate.

ANSWERS TO THE STUDY QUESTION

One answer to the question 'To what extent and for whom is childcare a barrier to work entry for lone parents?' was obtained at the end of Chapter 6. A quarter of interviewees were identified for whom childcare cost was the principle barrier to work entry. The characteristics of these parents are typical of lone parents out of work. Hardly any received maintenance or had qualifications above 'O' level and nearly all were tenants. They were disproportionately likely to be under 25 years of age and to have a child under 11 years.

These were parents who would need to pay for childcare in work but could not match the hours and rate of pay of a job vacancy to a childcare source they could then afford. Their problem – being 'unable to afford childcare' – does not place blame on either their earning potential or the cost of childcare but on their ability to reconcile the two. The solution will come from further subsidising childcare costs or wages or increasing lone parents earning potential and/or their income from maintenance payments.

More highly-skilled parents, in receipt of maintenance, with greater work experience are evidently better able to reconcile work and childcare. Importantly though, not all do. While nearly all those for whom childcare affordability posed the major barrier were out of work, so were half of those for whom it was not. These were parents who were as yet unable to contemplate time apart from their children or who lacked a motivation to take up work even in the presence of cheap or free childcare. These are not problems which changes in the affordability or availability of childcare can directly solve.

If the question is rephrased 'How much of a barrier to employment is childcare for lone parents?' the answer varies again depending on who is being discussed. It may be the only barrier at the margins, but it is a high one. And the margins of work are very wide for lone parents: unaffordable childcare keeps a third of out-of-work lone parents out of employment and half of these are in severe hardship as a result.

Two other small groups faced slightly different childcare problems. Some could not locate appropriate childcare. Although there was no evidence from these accounts that lone mothers faced an acute shortage of childcare, there was evidence that parents could not guarantee the availability of affordable childcare. For a small group, childcare cost is part of a larger barrier to employment dominated by other in-work costs. Tackling childcare may or may not reduce the barrier sufficiently to permit work entry.

Thus childcare posed some part of the problem to work entry for more than half the respondents out of work. Childcare was not a problem for the majority in work, even though the sample of workers were selected on the basis that they all paid for childcare. Childcare was a price 'career' women were prepared to pay to achieve the social, financial and career benefits work offered them. Others, for whom the financial rewards from work were fewer, had found jobs with hours which fitted the low-cost childcare they had available. Still others, who saw work offering neither financial nor social returns sufficient to motivate them, were out of work. Their social world revolved around their home and family, a world in which the use of childcare carried little salience. *They* did the childcare. It *was* their job.

A final answer to the question of the childcare barrier is how much of a difference the childcare disregard may make. The more lone parents are aware of it, know how it works and realise that it applies to them, the more it should help those for whom childcare costs pose a problem. For it to help others, its effects must be felt far more widely. The availability of the disregard may result in improved supply and availability of affordable care. It may broaden the legitimacy of the work and childcare combination, and bring greater awareness of its financial benefits, to lone parents. A disregard with an enlarged constituency, allowing 11, 12 and 13 year-olds the care their parents think they need, will enable many to enter work earlier than at present, and others to continue in work as their children enter their teenage years.

Note

1   Up from 15 per cent in 1991 to 21 per cent in 1993 and 26 per cent in 1994.

Annex A

THE DEPTH STUDY DESIGN

The aim of the depth interview study was to determine the position occupied by childcare among the labour market barriers of lone parents. In particular it set out to identify for whom policy initiatives aimed at reducing the cost of childcare will have an effect.

The principle policy initiative was launched in October 1994, just as the fieldwork began on the National Survey reported above. A disregard on childcare costs became available to claimants of in-work benefits – Family Credit, Council Tax Benefit, Housing Benefit – who have a child aged under 11 years of age and who pay for formal childcare while working. Those who might be eligible for such a disregard include lone parents with children aged under 11 years, and these formed the majority of depth interviewees.

However, another group has been identified for whom childcare needs persist well beyond their children's eleventh birthday. In considering the role of the childcare disregard, the Social Security Advisory Committee (SSAC) expressed concern that children with disabilities might present additional care demands, not addressed by policy if they were 11 years or older (SSAC, 1994). The ability of lone parents of children with disabilities to remain in work might be jeopardised by the loss of the disregard at age 11 years. An additional sample of such parents was included in the depth interview sample. A depth interview study of 57 lone parents followed up a sub-sample of the National Survey respondents. Data from the first survey was used to pinpoint lone parents at appropriate stages of labour market entry.

Experienced depth interviewers were briefed to explore thoroughly with lone mothers the role played by childcare and its cost in the decision made by respondents to work or not. The purpose of interviews was to try to determine exactly the role of the cost and availability of childcare in influencing how lone mothers perceived their employment opportunities and how they made their decisions to work or not. The topic guide was based on hypotheses established as tentative answers from the National Survey to six questions linking lone parents' perceptions of access to childcare and their work behaviour:

1. *Becoming a lone parent affects a woman's ability and willingness to work:* Economic activity is generally seen to be lower among lone parents than among other parents of dependent children. It is important to start at the individual level, however, to see how lone parents view the changes in circumstance which led up to their present status. Are they actually less inclined to work than if they had a partner, or than if they had not become a parent? In what ways do they see their prospects having changed as a result of becoming a lone parent?

2. *Childcare poses just one of many risks for lone parents considering entry into work:* It is often argued that moving off Income Support onto a mix of earnings from paid work and in-work benefits whilst paying for childcare, represents too much of a risk for lone parents of young children (Millar, Cooke and McLaughlin, 1989; Edwards, 1993). It will be necessary to identify how lone parents position components of a work, benefits and childcare package among these risks. Which do they consider most precarious or untenable?

3. *Potential work entrants must be confident of receiving a return from work using childcare which would justify the risks of entry into the labour market:* Lone parents are likely to have difficulty assessing fully the likely financial return from entering work, let alone the long-term or non-financial considerations which may enter into the decision.

   It is necessary to assess how realistically lone parents view paying for childcare. They may have to rely on many different childcare sources at any one time (for different children, at different times of day, and as back ups). How does cost enter the decision about the most appropriate sources of childcare? Are there indeed lone parents for whom using childcare is simply too costly to contemplate?

4. *Some lone parents will be unwilling to be separated from their children:* For some parents, being geographically separated from children who are being cared for by a stranger may create anxiety. Others may hold traditional views about looking after home and family. Over the short- to medium-term, such beliefs or fears may preclude entry into work.

5. *Some will not be able to match suitable job opportunities to affordable and acceptable childcare:* Work on the British Social Attitudes Survey of 1990 suggested that, given childcare arrangements of their choice, a quarter of mothers of young children working full-time would really prefer to work part-time (Witherspoon and Prior, 1991). Although two-thirds of mothers looking after the home when asked the same question were willing to enter work, only 13 per cent would choose to work full-time. It will be important to explore what underlies lone parents' preferences for hours of work each week. To what extent does childcare constrain their ability or likelihood of getting the jobs they would prefer?

6. *For some lone parents the decision rests less on the comparison of life in and out of work than on overcoming the financial, emotional and social challenges of the transition to work and using childcare:* Lone parents who move from being at home with their children to being at work and leaving their children with a formal carer face a major upheaval. How do they approach the process? Which elements create greatest anxiety?

Taken together, the answers to these questions should generate a detailed picture of lone parents' perceptions and expectations of life in work using childcare. Qualitative analysis will locate the motivations and intentions lone parents have for themselves and their families and give a clearer picture of the constraints they face in achieving their aims. The findings will aid explanation of the effectiveness of the new childcare disregard and also touch upon much broader concerns about lone parents' incentives and barriers to work that are sharply relevant to present policy considerations.

METHODS

The National Survey was used to identify small samples of lone mothers at different stages of entry into the labour market, to determine for whom the issue of childcare and work was relevant. The sample was drawn selectively from these respondents. These women were interviewed a second time between February and May 1995 using in-depth techniques.

- Sixty interviews were proposed and 57 completed with lone mothers who met the following criteria in October/November 1994: not permanently sick or disabled, not widowed, who had at least one dependent child in family, and whose income assessable for Family Credit purposes fell below the Family Credit minimum threshold[1] (£71.70), except where they were working 16 hours or more.[2]

- Sixteen interviews were planned (11 achieved, but see below) with those known to be out of work or working fewer than 16 hours a week, who had been seeking work in the past 12 months, had a youngest child aged between 5 and 11 years and who were not pregnant

- Sixteen interviews were planned (14 achieved) with lone parents who had started a job of 16 hours or more each week recently (during 1994), who used childcare and whose youngest was aged under 11 years

- Another 8 interviews were planned (13 achieved, see below) with lone parents who had not sought work of 16 hours or more in the previous 12 months.

- The sample sizes were regarded as targets, to be achieved once an allowance had been made for parents to have altered their employment status since the first interview.

The study was able to use the 1994 cross-section survey to particular advantage by selecting certain types of lone parent for second interview. It was not intended for the depth interview sample to be representative of lone parents as a whole, but to contain sufficient numbers in the groups outlined above for the study to explore particular issues in depth. For example, the study did not include lone parents who had been in their current job for more than one year. Thus the workers interviewed over-represented recent entrants to employment who had recently overcome their childcare problems in contemporary circumstances similar to those out of work. One of our stated hypotheses (after Millar, Cooke and McLaughlin, 1989) is that the transition from being out of work and on Income Support to full-time work using childcare is perceived as financially risky by lone parents. Such a sample enables us to explore how lone parents, known to have recent experience, managed the transition.

It was felt important to include the working group in order to compare the problems they have overcome with the problems seen by parents intending to work, and those that parents who do not intend to return to work still consider overwhelming.

A further sub-sample was selected who reported at least one of their children to have a long-standing illness or disability. These met the same criteria as for each of the above groups (sample sizes of 8, 8 and 4, respectively, 6, 7 and 6 achieved) but age restrictions on the age of the youngest child were lifted. These parents face a similarly structured problem deciding whether to enter work while paying for childcare. They would, however, be expected to have greater problems finding (and paying for) suitable childcare. A similar topic list to the main interviews was devised, but with interviewers placing a greater emphasis on relationship between the age of the child with disabilities and the extent of the constraint posed by access to childcare.

The raw response rates suggest that fewer work entrants were interviewed than anticipated: a total of 17 (11 without disabled children and six with) rather than 24. However, changes in employment status between the two interviews, and targeted top-up interviews meant that by time of second interview, the study had interviewed 22 work entrants. Eight of these work entrants had an ill or disabled child. As the balance was made up by non-workers who had entered work between the interviews, the top-up interview issued consisted largely of non-workers.

Topic guides reflected the six hypotheses ventured above. Three different guides were issued differing slightly according to the labour market status of the interviewee. The principal headings are given in Annex B. Interviews were clustered in four areas:

- *North West:* Cheshire, Greater Manchester, Lancashire, Merseyside
- *Midlands:* Nottinghamshire, Staffordshire, Warwickshire, West Midlands
- *South East:* Berkshire, Kent, Greater London, Hampshire, Hertfordshire
- *Scotland:* Grampian, Strathclyde, Tayside.

A single follow-up survey of these three groups was favoured over an extended longitudinal design, or one which involved only parents found able to sustain paid work over an extended period. There are important differences in the characteristics of lone parents found able to maintain work of 16 hours or more and those found out of work. Workers are more likely to own their own homes, occupy a higher socio-economic group, to have older children and to have once been married (McKay and Marsh, 1994). The PSI/DSS cohort study 1991–1995 (and ongoing) also suggests relatively little movement in the short-term between the two employment statuses, and hence little change in employment status for a longitudinal study to follow up.

Qualitative data analysis works to permit assumptions and hypotheses about the interaction between lone parents' perceptions about work and childcare and their labour market behaviour to be confirmed or denied (or *grounded)* in the data. The analysis was undertaken using text analysis grids, a well-established analytical technique. Following repeated reading of interview transcripts to discern principal themes, coded excerpts and summaries are transferred to two-way grids. Cases are entered on grid rows against thematic column headings. The concurrence of accounts and the extent of differentiation by respondent characteristics determines the applicability of hypotheses.

Findings from the Depth Study constitute the majority of Chapters 3–9 in the report. The structure follows the order of hypotheses and topic guides in first setting the context in which lone parents differentially affected by the cost and availability of childcare can be identified.

Notes

1   The amount of assessable income below which the family is entitled to the maximum Family Credit payment. When assessable income exceeds this threshold, the maximum Family Credit payment is reduced by 70 per cent of the difference between the assessable income total and the threshold.

2   This last condition had the effect of excluding lone parents who would be very unlikely to qualify for a childcare disregard even if they were to take up work of 16 hours or more. To achieve an assessable income above £71.70 each week would require high earnings from a part-time job, a substantial weekly maintenance payment or a high income from savings. Those with savings of more than £8,000 were also excluded from depth interviews.

Annex B

Topic Guide Headings

FAMILY RESOURCES

Determine major changes in work and family since last interview.
1   Family composition
2   Family and work history
3   Income strategy
4   Family and work in the future

PAID EMPLOYMENT

5   Conditions at work (workers only)
6   Returning to work

CHILDCARE

7   Requirement for childcare in work
8   Current use of childcare
9   Attitudes towards childcare
10   Knowledge of locally available childcare
11   General attitudes towards women and work, child(ren) in childcare

For clarity, sub-headings have been omitted

BIBLIOGRAPHY

Baldwin, S (1985) *The Costs of Caring: Families with Disabled Children.* London: Routledge and Kegan Paul.

Beresford, B (1995) *Positively Parents: Caring for a Severely Disabled Child.* London: HMSO.

Berger, M C and Black, D A (1992) 'Child care subsidies, quality of care and the labour supply of low-income, single mothers', *Review of Economics and Statistics,* 24, pp.635–642.

Blundell, R (1994) 'Work incentives and labour supply in the UK', in Bryson and McKay (eds.) op. cit., pp.19–38.

Bowlby, J (1964) *Child care and the Growth of Love.* Harmondsworth: Penguin.

Bradshaw, J and Millar, J (1991) *Lone Parent Families in the UK.* London: HMSO.

Bryson, A and McKay, S (eds) (1994) *Is It Worth Working?* London: PSI.

Bryson, A and McKay, S (1994) 'Is it worth working? An introduction to some of the issues'. In A Bryson and S McKay (eds) op. cit.

Clarke-Stewart, A (1980) 'Observation and experiment: complementary strategies for studying day care and social development'. In S Kilmer (ed.) *Advances in Early Education and Day Care.* Greenwich CT: JAI Press.

Coleman, D and Salt, J (1993) *The British Population.* Oxford: Oxford University Press.

Connelly, R (1992) 'The effect of childcare costs on married women's labour force participation', *Review of Economics and Statistics*, 24, pp.83–90.

Department of Social Security (1995) *Social Security Departmental Report*. London: HMSO.

Duncan, A. (1990) *Labour Supply Decisions and Non-Convex Budget Sets*. Working Paper W90/7. London: IFS.

Duncan, A, Giles, C and Webb, S (1995) *The Impact of Subsidising Childcare*. Manchester: Equal Opportunities Commission.

Edwards, R (1993) 'Taking the initiative: the government, mothers and day care provision', *Critical Social Policy*, pp.36–50.

Finlayson, L, Ford, R and Marsh, A, 'Paying more for childcare', *Labour Market Trends*, July 1996, pp.295–303.

Ford, R, Marsh, A and Finlayson, L (1996 forthcoming) *What happens to lone parents*. London: PSI.

Ford, R, Marsh, A and McKay, S (1995) *Changes in Lone Parenthood*. London: HMSO.

Furnham A and Bochner S (1986) *Culture Shock: Psychological reactions to unfamiliar environments*. London: Methuen.

Holtermann, S (1992) *Investing in Young Children: costing an Education and Day Care Service*. London: National Children's Bureau.

Holtermann, S (1993) *Becoming a Breadwinner: policies to assist lone parents with childcare*. London: Daycare Trust.

Joshi, H and Davies, H (1993) 'Mothers' human capital and childcare in Britain', *National Institute Economic Review*, November 1993.

Kozak, M (1994) *Not Just Nine to five: A survey of shift workers' childcare needs*. London: Daycare Trust.

Laidler, D (1981) *Introduction to microeconomics*. Oxford: Philip Allan.

Leeming A, Unell, J and Walker, R (1994) *Lone mothers*. London: HMSO.

Marsh, A (1994) 'The benefit fault line', In M White (ed), op. cit., pp.64–79.

Marsh, A and McKay, S (1993a) 'Families, work and the use of child-care', *Employment Gazette,* August, pp.361–370.

Marsh, A and McKay S (1993b) *Families, Work and Benefits.* London: PSI.

Marsh, A, Ford, R and Finlayson, L (1996 forthcoming) *Lone Parents, Work and Benefits.* London: PSI.

Mayall, B and Petrie, P (1983) *Childminding and Day Nurseries: What kind of care?* London: Heinemann Educational.

McKay, S and Marsh, A (1994) *Lone Parents and Work.* London: HMSO.

Meltzer, H (1994) *Day Care Services for Children.* London: HMSO.

Millar, J, Cooke, K and McLaughlin, E (1989) 'The employment lottery: risk and social security benefits', *Policy and Politics,* 17, pp.75–81.

Philp, M and Duckworth, D (1982) *Children with disabilities and their families.* Windsor: NFER-Nelson.

Sanderson, I and Percy-Smith, J [with Ann Foreman, Melissa Wraight, Liam Murphy and Pat Petrie] (1995) *The Out-of-School Childcare Grant Initiative.* Sheffield: Employment Department.

Scott, J and Duncombe, J (1991) 'A cross-national comparison of gender-role attitudes: is the working mother selfish?' Working Papers of the ESRC Research Centre on Micro-social change. Paper 9. Colchester: University of Essex.

Sly, F (1994) 'Mothers in the labour market', *Employment Gazette,* November, pp.403–413.

Social Security Advisory Committee (1994) *In work – out of work: the role of incentives in the benefits system.* The Review of Social Security Paper 1. Leeds: BA Publishing.

Smith, F (1995) *The Absent Child,* Geographical Paper 116. Department of Geography, University of Reading.

White, M ed (1994) *Unemployment and Public Policy in a Changing Labour Market.* London: PSI.

Witherspoon, S and Prior, G (1991) 'Working mothers: free to choose?' In R Jowell and B Taylor (eds) *British Social Attitudes: the eighth report.* Aldershot: Gower.